Cover design: *Ka Pika Pua o Hale Ali'i, King's Flower Vase. This quilt pattern was influenced by the etched glass design on the bottom of the 'Iolani Palace doors.*

Courtesy of Grove Farm, Kaua'i, Hawai'i.

George E. Bacon

Sheet crystal door panels were made in England and designed and etched in San Francisco for the massive front and rear portals of the Palace. The Hawaiian Consul in San Francisco, Henry W. Severance, in 1881 wrote a bit apprehensively to the Minister of Foreign Affairs in Honolulu: "The workmen who executed the figured glass, are inclined to decorate profusely but I have tried to keep them within limits. I hope in your judgment they have not exceeded the bounds of good taste in the figures represented. In the large Transom lights which have the coat of arms, I wished to have the Taro leaf introduced, which is similar to the leaf of the Calla lily, but in making the same they have added the flower. I shall be glad to know that you approve all the work."

TABLE OF CONTENTS

THE HISTORY OF 'IOLANI PALACE
POTLUCK PARTIES

Potluck parties are a new tradition at 'Iolani Palace. The first one was held on an evening in November of 1977 to celebrate the 141st anniversary of King Kalākaua's birthday. It was organized and enjoyed by the first class of volunteer docents, at 'Iolani Palace and in the process formed close friendships.

Their inaugural Potluck Party was a delightfully informal affair. Tables were set up on the Diamond Head side of the Barracks. Long extension cords snaked from the desk of Friends' Secretary Helen Rantala in the Barracks, through a window and out to the tables, where her desk lamp provided a fluorescent glow. Each participant brought a favorite dish, and so abundant was the repast that all passersby, including the State Capitol Guards, were invited to join the party.

During the evening John Lake's Hula Halau performed beneath the shadowing trees, transporting those watching back to the monarchy days. The moonlit Palace created the perfect backdrop for the dancers and added to the aura of the 1880s.

The 1977 Potluck Party was such a success and provided so many happy memories that it was repeated the following year, this time as a birthday celebration for former Board Member and Cookbook Editor Henry Piltz Kramer, one of the first of the Palace Docents and Greeters. Since then the Docents have held a Potluck Party every three months, to celebrate birthdays and other special events. The biggest Potluck of them all is held at Christmas. Then the extended volunteer family, the Palace 'Ohana, joins in.

Over the years a number of imaginative Potluck Parties have been held and at each one favorite recipes have been exchanged among the members of the Palace 'Ohana. Now, in the spirit of sharing, which is so much a part of the Hawaiian and the Palace tradition, the Palace 'Ohana wishes to share our Potluck recipes with all of you.

Na Lei Kukui O Ka Haleali'i

The Volunteers and Friends of 'Iolani Palace

ACKNOWLEDGEMENTS

For Their Assistance And Support

The Board of Directors of The Friends of 'Iolani Palace
Abigail K. Kawananakoa, President

The King Kalakaua Jubilee Centennial Celebration Committee
Mary Helen Styan, Chairperson

The Staff of The Friends of 'Iolani Palace
Alice F. Guild, Managing Director
H.J. Bartels, Curator
Corinne Chun, Assistant Curator
June Bradley, Palace Shop Manager
Darryl K. Cabacungan, Volunteer Coordinator
Stuart W.H. Ching, Education Coordinator

Palace Greeters, Docents and Guardians
Henry Piltz Kramer, Cookbook Editor
Mary Reed Hughes, Coordinator and Typist
Kulia Alec Toomey, Cover Design Consultant
Bea Billings, Ann Jurczynski, Dorothy Kendall
Olive Linde, Sally McClellan, Proofreaders

Cover Design Courtesy of
Grove Farm, Kaua'i, Hawai'i

First Printing – November, 1987
Second Printing – April, 1988
Third Printing – February, 1989
Fourth Printing – October, 1989

4

Breakfast at Iolani Palace

IN HONOR OF

Mr. Edmund C. Atkinson

GRAND MASTER OF MASONS OF CALIFORNIA

AND

Mrs. Atkinson

MONDAY, JUNE 13, 1887

Menu

FRUITS

POISSONS

Mullet   Kumu

VIANDES ET VOLAILLES

Beefsteak   Maintenon Cutlets   Brain   Salmi of Ducks

GIBIER

Squabs on Toast   Broiled Chicken

SHRIMP CURRY   SALADE et FROMAGE

OMELETTE a la NESSELRODE

DESSERT   ICE CREAM

Cafe   The   Chocolat

PUPUS AND APPETIZERS

KUKANA BOURKE'S ARTICHOKE CHEESE DIP

1 cup mayonnaise
2 cups shredded
   mozzarella cheese
2 8 oz. cans artichoke hearts,
   drained and chopped
   (or 2 jars marinated hearts)

1 tsp. garlic powder
2 cups grated Parmesan cheese
1 tsp. paprika

Wheat crackers

In a 1½ quart casserole dish, combine the mayo, cheeses, artichoke hearts and garlic powder.

Sprinkle with paprika. Bake at 350° uncovered for 25 minutes. Serve hot with wheat crackers.

Suzie Anderson

ITALIAN PUPU DIP

1 round loaf unsliced French bread, hollowed out,
   making cubes for dip
1 pkg. cooked frozen spinach, well drained
1 can chopped water chestnuts
2 cups sour cream or plain yogurt
1 cup mayonnaise
1 pkg. dry vegetable soup mix (Knorr's is good)

Mix. Chill 4 hours. Serve in hollowed out bread using cut outs for dip.

Jeanne Read Alden

HIKIWALE (easy) POPCORN SPRINKLE

1 env. (1.4 oz.) dry buttermilk salad dressing mix
1 env. (¾ oz.) instant dry tomato soup mix
⅓ cup dry grated American or Parmesan cheese
½ tsp. onion salt

Mix all ingredients thoroughly. Sprinkle amount desired over buttered popcorn. Keep mixture in an airtight container between uses. Makes ¾ cup.

Suzie Anderson

LOMI SALMON

10 ripe tomatoes	1 lb. raw salted salmon
2 tbsp. blended limu-kohu	1 whole round onion
¼ bunch green leaf onion	

Dunk 6 tomatoes into boiling water for 2 seconds. Soak in ice cold water 12 seconds. Peel and remove skin of tomatoes. Dice and put into blender with 2 tbsp. limu-kohu. Liquify and place into a bowl. Place in freezer until ready to use. Then defrost.

Dice 1 round onion. Place into bowl. Chop ¼ bunch green leaf onion into finely cut squares. Place in bowl. Dice 4 tomatoes into small squares. Place in bowl.

Slice 1 lb. raw salted salmon into 4 parts and soak in fresh water. Rinse. Resoak 3 times. Let soak 20 min. Rinse. Dice into small fine squares. Place into huge bowl. Add all other ingredients. Serve cold with poi.

Judy Parrish

CREAM CHEESE WUN TUN PI

1 16 oz. pkg. cream cheese
1 6½ oz. can crab, drain well
2 tbsp. chopped green onion
2 pkgs. wun tun pi shells

Cream the cheese, crab and green onion. Fill each shell with ½ tsp. of mixture. Fold shell into a triangle, sealing edges with water. Join 2 corners on folded side, again moistening with water. There is no fast rule as to how the shells should be folded as long as the mixture is sealed. Fry in deep hot oil until shells turn golden brown.

Makes around 50.

Rosemary Eberhardt

SAUSAGE-CHEESE APPETIZERS

1 lb. hot sausage, or Portuguese sausage*
1 lb. cheddar cheese grated
3 cups Bisquick

Crumble the sausage. Add cheese and mix well. Blend in Bisquick. Shape into walnut-size balls and bake on cooky sheets for 20 minutes at 350°. These can be frozen and reheated in a 350° oven. Makes 75-90.

*If Portuguese sausage is used it must be skinned and fat removed.

Mary Reed Hughes

PINEAPPLE CHEESE LOG

2 8 oz. pkgs. cream cheese, softened
1 8½ oz. can crushed pineapple, drained
2 cups chopped pecans or macadamia nuts
¼ cup finely chopped green peppers
1 tbsp. dried onion flakes
1 tbsp. seasoned salt

In medium bowl beat cheese until soft. Add 1 cup nuts and remaining ingredients, mix. Roll onto remaining nuts. Wrap in foil and chill. Makes 3 small rolls. Serve with crackers.

Mary Reed Hughes

CHEESE PUFFS

1 cup shredded sharp
  cheddar cheese
½ cup butter
1 cup rice krispies

1 cup flour
½ tsp. Tabasco
⅛ tsp. pepper
⅛ tsp. salt

Mix. Pinch off. Bake on cooky sheet at 350° for 10-15 minutes. Mix with hands, pressing dough together. Break off and shape ball size of large marbles. Does not spread when baking. Flatten on cooky sheet with thumb. Lightly grease cooky sheet. Makes approximately 100.

Mary Reed Hughes

CHEESE SPREAD

1 stick margarine   1 jar Old English cheese spread
1 small pkg. Roquefort cheese   1 large pkg. cream cheese

Have all ingredients at room temperature. Mix with electric beater. Add to taste a few dashes of Worcestershire sauce, garlic, Tabasco. Chill and serve. Keeps well. Makes 1 large cheese ball.

Jean St. John

CRAB SPREAD

Mix well: 8 oz. cream cheese
          1 tsp. minced onion
          1 tbsp. lemon juice
          ¾ cup mayonnaise
Add: 1 6 oz. can crabmeat

Beat 1 egg and mix all together. Put in small buttered baking dishes. Sprinkle with grated Parmesan cheese and paprika. Bake at 350° for 25 minutes. Serve immediately with crackers.

Dawn Krause

ARTICHOKE-CHEESE SPREAD

1 can artichoke hearts, chopped and drained
1 cup Parmesan cheese, grated
1 cup mayonnaise
Dash of garlic salt

Mix all ingredients. Place in baking dish and bake at 400° for 10 minutes. Serve with crackers.

Erla Pauole

NORIMAKI SUSHI WITH HOT DOGS

1 cup uncooked rice
1 piece kombu (2-3 inches) – Japanese seaweed
4 tbsp. rice vinegar
2 tbsp sugar – to taste
½ tsp. salt

Wash rice, drain, let stand for 1 hour. Bring rice, water and kombu to a boil. Remove kombu. Cover rice and finish cooking. Let stand.

Boil together vinegar, sugar and salt.

Put rice on wooden tray, sprinkle with vinegar mix and toss. Fan rice to cool it quickly to lukewarm.

Norimaki:

Sudare (bamboo mat)
2 eggs
1 tbsp. shoyu
Cooked beef hot dogs – slit
   lengthwise and fill with a
   little mustard and relish
2 tsp. peanut oil

Takuwan – cut in strips
1½ tsp. wasabi powder mixed
   with water to make paste
3-4 sheets nori
2 tbsp. sugar
½ tsp. salt
1 small cucumber

Beat eggs with salt. Heat 1 tsp. oil and fry ½ of egg until firm. Remove to plate. Fry other half. Let cool then slice into ½ in. strips.

Peel cucumber – cut in ½ lengthwise. Remove seeds and cut into lengthwise strips.

Dampen sudare, place sheet of nori on it. Press sushi rice onto nori leaving about 1 in. clear on edges nearest and furthest from you. Rice should be about ½ in. thick. Add egg strips, hot dogs, takuwan strips, cucumber strips lightly smeared with wasabi paste. Start with edge nearest you and roll all into jelly roll formation using sudare to shape and press even and firm. Let sit 2 minutes. Slice with a sharp wet knife into desired slices.

I suggest you double or triple the recipe to make it worthwhile. This sushi goes fast!

Rhoda Napoleon

DILL WEED DIP

1 cup sour cream
1½ tbsp. onion flakes
1 tbsp. dill weed

1½ tsp. Beau Monde seasoning
1 cup mayonnaise
1½ tbsp. parsley flakes

Combine ingredients and use as dip for veggies or chips.

Luana McKenney

HOT CRAB DIP MARY

8 oz. cream cheese, softened
1 can crab
2 tbsp. milk
¼ tsp. salt

2 tbsp. minced onion
½ tsp. horseradish
Pepper to taste

Mix ingredients. Place in small oven proof dish suitable for serving. Sprinkle with 1 can French fried onion rings. Bake uncovered at 375° for 15 minutes until bubbly. Serve with crackers. A winner!

Luana McKenney

SPINACH DIP

2 pkgs. frozen chopped spinach (Squeeze out water)
2 cups sour cream
1 pkg. Knorr's onion soup mix
1 can minced clams, drained
1 can water chestnuts, chopped
1 cup mayonnaise

Mix thoroughly and chill. Serve with monkey bread from the Prize Bakery, 2295 N. King St., Honolulu.

Or serve with crackers, toasted bread, etc.

Tsuruko A. Ohye

NACHOS – HOT PUPU

Spread 1 package of Doritos corn chips on cooky sheet.

Shred 1 block of medium or sharp cheddar cheese and sprinkle generously over chips.

Place in oven at 300° for about 5 minutes or until cheese has melted.

Sprinkle taco sauce over top and serve.

Flodie VanOrden

EASY CHEESE LAVOSH

Break a package of lavosh into pieces. Place on baking sheet. Top with slices of sharp cheddar cheese. Broil 2 minutes. Serve hot.

Mary Reed Hughes

PIROSHKI (RUSSIAN)

2 eggs	2 cakes yeast
flour	1 tsp. salt
1 cup warm milk	2 tbsp. melted butter

Dissolve the yeast cakes in the milk. Add enough flour to make a thick batter. Stir well. Put in warm place to rise. When it has risen add salt, butter and beaten eggs and enough flour to make a fairly thick dough. Knead well and let rest once more. Roll out dough to ⅛ inch on floured board. Cut round or square pieces. Fill with ground meat (fish, boiled rice or fried cabbage). Fold in two and press edges firmly together. Bake at 450° until brown, or if preferred, fry in deep fat until brown.

Meat Filling:

Brown 1 finely chopped onion in 1 tbsp. butter. Add some very finely chopped meat (beef, veal, lamb, pork, chicken). Season with salt and pepper and cook a short while. When cold fill into piroshki as described. Especially good at Christmas.

Brian Miller

SOUR CREAM HERRING

1 12 oz. jar Lasco Brand Spiced Cut Herring
1 8 oz. container sour cream
1 medium Maui onion
4 medium Kosher tiny dill pickles
1 small-medium tart apple
3 heaping tsp. mayonnaise
2-3 level tsp. sugar

Dice herring, onion, pickles, apple and combine in bowl. Add remaining ingredients and mix well.

Refrigerate. Serve with peasant bread, French bread or crackers.

Corinne Chun

SEAFOOD SPREAD

This dip or spread is simple and quick to make. It may be made ahead of time and heated in a 350° oven for 20-25 minutes or until lightly browned.

1 tbsp. butter
2 stalks celery, fine chopped
½ green pepper, finely chopped
1 tbsp. Worcestershire sauce
¾ cup mayonnaise
1 tbsp. lemon juice
1 6½ oz. can crabmeat, flaked
1 6½ oz. can shrimp
¼ tsp. salt (optional)
½ tsp. pepper (optional)
¼ cup chopped onions (optional)
6 saltines or soda crackers, crushed
¼ cup Parmesan cheese, grated

Saute celery, green pepper, Worcestershire sauce and onions in butter until vegetables are tender. Add mayonnaise. Pour lemon juice over shrimp and crabmeat and add to first mixture. Put into greased casserole and top with crushed saltines and cheese. Dot with butter and bake. Serves 8 as hors d'oeuvre. Serves 6 as luncheon dish.

Mary Helen Hooululahui Styan

HANNAH'S DELIGHT STUFFED CHICKEN PUPUS

5 lb. box chicken
1 large carrot, cut in strips
½ bunch watercress,
    cut and steamed
1 kamaboko fish cake
    (pink and white) cut in
    thin strips

1 box round toothpicks
1 round fish cake, cut in thin strips
Salt and pepper
Garlic and ginger
1½ cups oil

Cut all ingredients and debone chicken. Place chicken on chopping board. Add salt and pepper. Add 1 strip of each ingredient and roll. Stick toothpick in to fasten. Place garlic and ginger in oil. Deep fry in wok about 5 to 7 minutes or to golden brown.

PORK HASH, WON TON PI and bowl of water

Place pork hash on won ton pi and seal with water. Fry in same oil as stuffed chicken. Serve with Chinese mustard. Serves 10-15.

                            Samuel Kaliko Sin Kui Ah Yuen, Jr.

WELSH RAREBIT

1 lb. grated cheddar cheese
½ tbsp. butter
1 egg, slightly beaten

2 tsp. Worcestershire sauce
½ cup beer
½ tsp. dry mustard

Heat cheese and beer over *very* low heat until cheese melts. Add seasonings, add egg and continue to stir until mixture thickens and is creamy.

Serve on toast over bacon and tomatoes. Serves 4.

                                            Mary Kirkham

SOUPS

MY GODMOTHER'S QUICK PORTUGUESE BEAN SOUP

2 big cans of cheap
  pork and beans

2 small ham hocks
2 chopped medium onions

Boil the ham hocks and onions until tender. Remove ham from bones and add to beans. Add shell macaroni, 4 oz. Portuguese sausage, sliced; potatoes, tomatoes. Add water if needed. Serves 4.

Barbara Pualani Lake

TOFU AND SPINACH SOUP

Chicken broth plus water to –
  1 cup per person
1 piece salted turnip
  (chung choy)

½ piece tofu cake
Bone from pork butt plus
  chunks of pork
1 bunch fresh spinach

Rinse turnip. Add to broth with bone and meat. Bring to boil and simmer for 30 minutes. Add spinach and cook for 20 minutes. Add tofu bits and cook another 10 minutes. Serve with drop of sesame oil.

Mary Nickel

HAMBURGER SOUP

1½ lb. ground chuck
2 tbsp. oil
¼ tsp. each oregano, basil,
  pepper
⅛ tsp. savory salt
1 pkg. onion soup mix
6 cups hot water

1 8 oz. can tomato sauce
1 tbsp. soy sauce
1 cup celery, sliced crosswise
¼ cup chopped celery leaves
1 cup sliced carrots
⅓ cup dried split peas
¾ cup small elbow macaroni

In large pot brown meat in oil. Drain off fat. Add salt, pepper, spices and dried onion soup mix. Stir in water, tomato sauce and soy sauce. cover and simmer 15 min. Add fresh vegetables to mixture and simmer about 30 min. Add peas. Cook for about 15 min. Add macaroni. Simmer about 30 min. longer. Add water if necessary.

Eleanor Azevedo

ZUCCHINI SOUP

Saute 1 chopped med. onion in 1 stick butter until wilted. Add 2 med. large zucchini thinly sliced. Peel but leave some peel on for color. Saute lightly.

Add 2½ cups chicken stock – may use bouillon dissolved in hot water. Simmer 15 min. or until tender. Whirl in blender until smooth. Add ¼ tsp. nutmeg, ¼ tsp. basil, salt and pepper to taste. If using bouillon, omit salt until tasting. Simmer 5 min. to combine flavors, stirring to prevent sticking. Add a dash of A-1 sauce and fold in finely chopped green pepper – about ¼ cup. If too thick, add a little milk or cream. Serve hot or cold.

Betty Bowyer

GRAND MARAIS FISH CHOWDER

Break 2½ lbs. fresh skinned fish, cut up. (Cod, trout, whatever.)

2 cups melted butter
1½ tsp. salt
1 tsp. curry powder
1 cup white wine – Sauterne
1 cup flour
½ tsp. pepper
½ gallon milk

Stir flour into melted butter using wire whip. Add salt, pepper and curry powder. Add the milk and wine. Stir until smooth.

Add fish to sauce. Cook very slowly. *Do not boil.*

Add parsley flakes. If desired, add peeled, diced cooked potatoes.

Helen V. Rantala

CLAM CHOWDER

2 cans baby clams
  (save the liquid)
6 slices bacon
5 med. potatoes, sliced
Salt and freshly ground pepper
1 qt. whole milk

1 tbsp. butter
2 tbsp. chopped parsley
2 med. onions, chopped
3 cups water, salted
1 cup cream
1 tsp. thyme

1. Fry bacon until crisp. Drain and crumble.
2. Strain the bacon fat into a clean skillet and add butter. Saute the onion until softened.
3. Cook the potatoes in salted water until very tender. Add with the cooking water to the onion. Add bacon bits. Add thyme.
4. Salt and pepper to taste. Bring to gentle boil. Reduce heat and simmer for about 5 minutes.
5. Add cream, parsley and clams. Add milk. Heat briefly and serve at once. It is important not to cook the clams too long for they will toughen quickly. Serves 8.

Beverly Hansen

GAZPACHO

3 cans whole tomatoes,
  drained (about 6 cups)
1 onion, chopped
½-1 cup cucumber, chopped
½ tsp. ground cumin
Freshly ground pepper

¼ cup olive oil
½ cup green pepper, chopped
1 clove garlic, minced
1 tbsp salt
2 cups V-8 juice
¼-½ cup white wine vinegar

Garnish: ½ cup each of chopped onion, green pepper and cucumber

1. Put the tomatoes, onion, green pepper, cucumber and spices in a blender or food processor and blend.
2. Transfer to a large bowl. Stir in the V-8 juice. If a very spicy taste is desired add 1 tsp. of Worcestershire sauce. Cover and chill.
3. Stir in oil and vinegar just before serving.
4. Serve with a topping of sour cream & chives.

Serves 10.

Beverly Hansen

PRINCESS RUTH'S PORTUGUESE BEAN SOUP

2 cups red beans
1 lb. ham hocks
A few sprigs parsley
1 onion, chopped
1 Portuguese sausage,
    hot or mild

1 head cabbage
2 lge. potatoes
3 carrots
1 cup celery
1 16 oz. can whole tomatoes
2 cloves garlic

Cover kidney beans with cold water and soak overnight. Cook until done – about 1 hour. Cover ham hocks with water and cook until meat comes easily off the bones. Put in garlic, 1 bay leaf, onion salt while ham hocks are boiling. Discard the bones.

Chop up parsley, onion, sausage, potatoes, carrots, celery. Add them along with tomatoes to the beans that are already tender. Pour in at this time the ham hock stock and meat. Cook until done, simmering about an hour and stirring frequently.

Just before the potatoes are soft, add salt and a little black pepper. Add water as desired. Otherwise it might be too thick. Finally add the cabbage and maybe a cup of macaroni. Serves 12.

Suzie Anderson

EGG DROP SOUP

2 slices pork (½ lb., plus bones)
2 eggs, beaten with a little salt
1 piece salted turnip (chung choy)
¼ bag bean sprout
Chicken broth plus water to equal 1 cup per person

Cut meat into small pieces. Marinate in 1 tbsp. soy sauce, ½ tsp. cornstarch, 1 tsp. oil, a little Ajinomoto. Wash and cut turnip into bite size pieces. Heat soup pot with 1 tbsp. oil. Brown bean sprouts and remove. Put broth, turnip and bone in pot and bring to boil. Add meat chunks and cook on high for 10 min. Reduce heat, add bean sprouts and cook another 15-20 min. Have beaten eggs ready. Remove from heat. Add eggs while stirring. Remove bones and serve.

Mary Nickel

CABBAGE SOUP

½ head cabbage, chopped
1 lge. onion, chopped
1 tbsp. salt
4 allspice berries
1 lb. ground beef

6 cups water
3 tbsp. sugar
1 bay leaf
2 peppercorns
2 6 oz. cans tomato paste

Combine all ingredients except tomato paste in a large saucepan. Bring to boil. Lower heat and simmer 20-30 minutes. Add tomato paste and cook 15 minutes longer. Freezes well. Makes 2 quarts.

Jean St. John

VICHYSSOISE

1 lge. onion, sliced
4 lge. leeks (use only the
  white parts, slice)
2 tbsp. butter
5 med. sized potatoes,
  peeled and sliced

1 qt. chicken broth
1 tbsp. salt
2 cups half and half
2 cups milk
1 cup heavy cream

1. Saute the onion and leeks in the butter over low heat until they soften.
2. Add the potatoes, chicken broth and salt.
3. Bring to a boil, cover, reduce heat and simmer gently for 35 to 40 minutes or until the potatoes are very soft.
4. Rub the mixture through a fine sieve.
5. Return to the heat. Add the milk and half and half. Season to taste. Slowly bring the mixture to a boil, stirring constantly.
6. Cool the soup. Rub again through a fine sieve.
7. Place in the refrigerator in a covered container. Allow mixture to become very cold.
8. Stir in the heavy cream.
9. Served with chopped chives on the surface of each cup.

Serves 10.

Beverly Hansen

FRENCH ONION SOUP

5 to 6 large onions slice half-moon.

Brown onions in butter in heavy pot. Add beef stock or broth. Simmer to taste. For more flavor add 1 pkg. of Lipton onion soup mix.

Kimberly Garner

PAPAYA SOUP

1 med. papaya (green, with slightly yellow)
½ lb. sparerib (boil first to remove fat)
2 oz. raw peanuts - 4 tbsp. - unsalted
Water - 1 cup per person

Peel papaya. Cut into chunky bite sizes. Rinse peanuts. Brown sparerib in 1 tbsp. oil. Place water in pot. Add peanuts and bring to boil (add a little salt). Boil the spare rib, peanuts, with salt, for 20 minutes on medium heat. Add papaya chunks. Bring to boil on high heat. Turn to low and cook another 20 minutes. Add soy sauce when served.

Mary Nickel

MAMA'S SOUP BONE

2 large size soup bones
1 piece about 1½ lb. belly pork, diced bite size
2 pkgs. dried kidney beans soaked overnight and picked over

Boil soup bone until tender, almost falling off bone. Add pork. Simmer. Boil kidney beans in another large pot until tender. Add to soup bone and pork. Simmer till thickens. Serves 6 people with bread and good vegetable salad.

Victoria Niihau

NOTES

SALADS

CURRY CHICKEN SALAD

Season 3 cups diced chicken with:

1½ tsp. salt	¼ tsp. pepper
½ cup diced celery	1 cup diced apple
2 tsp. grated onion	

Blend:

1 tsp. curry powder	1 cup mayonnaise
¼ cup heavy cream	

Pour into chicken mixture and mix well.

Excellent served in half a papaya with mango chutney as a topping.

Beverly Schulte

BEET SALAD

1 pkg. strawberry jello	1 pkg. raspberry jello
1 pkg. cherry jello	4 cups boiling water
1 can #303 Julienne beets	1 can #2 crushed pineapple
½ cup sweet pickle juice	

Dissolve the 3 kinds of jello in the boiling water. Drain beets and pineapple (approximately 1½ cups) and add this to pickle juice. Add to dissolved gelatin mixture. Chill. Stir in beets and pineapple and chill until firm.

Prepare dressing in order given and add cream if consistency needs it. Let stand several hours for the flavors to blend. Serves 16 people.

Dressing:

1 cup mayonnaise	Light cream
1 tbsp. chopped green pepper	1 tbsp. chopped green onions

Mae Barth

JANET'S SPINACH SALAD

2 bags spinach
2 cups water chestnuts, sliced
4 hard boiled eggs, chopped

½ lb. cooked bacon, crumbled
1 cup bean sprouts

Dressing:

1 cup salad oil
⅓ cup catsup
¼ cup apple cider vinegar

1 tbsp. Worcestershire sauce
¾ cup sugar
2 tsp. salt

Audrey Toopes

CURRIED SPINACH SALAD

2 bunches fresh spinach, washed and broken in pieces
3 red or golden apples, diced
⅔ cup Spanish peanuts
½ cup raisins
⅓ cup sliced green onions
2 tbsp. toasted sesame seeds

Curry Dressing:

Let stand at room temperature 2 hours:

½ cup white vinegar
⅔ cup salad oil
1 tsp. each: curry powder, salt, dry mustard
2-3 tbsp. finely chopped chutney
¼ tsp. Tabasco

Serves 6-8.

Claudean Rolison

PA'I PASTA SALAD

1 jar marinated artichoke hearts
⅛ cup vinegar and
   ¼ cup olive oil
1 can tuna
1 can mushrooms

Basil, oregano, parsley,
   garlic salt to taste
2 cups small sea shell pasta
1 can olives

Drain and reserve liquid from artichokes. Add to liquid approximately the above amounts of vinegar and oil. You should have about ¾ cup in all.

Mix tuna, olives, mushrooms and artichokes. Add dry herbs and garlic salt. Add liquid. Set aside.

Cook 2 cups pasta and mix everything together.

Cover and chill. Great to do the day before and let it sit!

Suzie Anderson
(from Donivee Laird)

BEAN SALAD

1 pkg. frozen lima beans
1 pkg. frozen wax beans

1 pkg. frozen green beans

Cook until tender or according to package directions. Drain, then put in bowl to cool.

Dressing:
Olive oil, wine vinegar, salt, pepper, garlic (fresh or powdered), parsley. Or use Italian dressing.

Pour enough dressing in bowl to cover all vegetables. Stir frequently. Marinate overnight in refrigerator. Serve cold.

Audrey Iwalani Vance

GERMAN POTATO SALAD

5 lbs. potatoes, cooked with skins on
½ lb. bacon, cut up
1 large onion, cut up

Saute bacon and onion together. Add:
¾ cup cider vinegar   ¾ cup sugar
¾ cup water

Bring to a boil. Thicken with cornstarch or flour.

Peel and slice potatoes. Add salt and pepper to taste. Pour warm sauce over and mix.

Audrey Toopes

For people who hate to cook!

CHICKEN SALAD

1 lge. can chunk white chicken
2 dozen white seedless grapes, cut in half
½ cup chopped celery
½ cup chopped walnuts
Mayonnaise to taste

Mix everything and serve on a quartered tomato.

Garnish with sliced hardboiled egg, carrot sticks and parsley.

Linda Norris

MARINATED CARROTS

2-3 lbs. carrots, sliced into bite size pieces
1 lge. onion, sliced into bite size pieces
1 lge. bell pepper, diced

Cook together until just tender. Drain. Add:
1 can tomato soup   ½ cup cooking oil
¼ cup vinegar   1 tsp. pepper
1 tsp. dry mustard   1 tsp. Worcestershire sauce

Marinate vegetables overnight in this dressing in a covered container in the refrigerator. Serve cold. Serves 6-8.

Helen Schlapak

SUPER SALAD

Salt and pepper as you go.

First layer: ½ head lettuce, torn into bite sizes
Second layer: 2½ cups cooked diced chicken
Third layer: 1 can water chestnuts, sliced
Fourth layer: lge. pkg. uncooked frozen green peas – rinse with cold water, drain.
Fifth layer: 1 pt. mayonnaise or sour cream (I mix it half and half) Little less than 2 tbsp. sugar
Sixth layer: 1 cup chopped celery. ½ cup green pepper
Seventh layer: ½ cup red onion, chopped
Eighth layer: 6 oz. grated cheddar cheese
Ninth layer: 7-10 slices bacon, fried crisp and crumbled
Tenth layer: 3-4 hard cooked eggs, chopped

Cover and refrigerate overnight. Serve with fresh fruit.

Jackie March

YUMMY SALAD

2 pkgs. Knox gelatin
¾ cup sugar
1 cup cottage cheese
2 cups crushed pineapple, undrained

½ cup water
½ cup grated cheese
1 bottle Avoset

Dissolve 2 pkgs. gelatin in ½ cup.

In pot put 2 cups crushed pineapple, undrained. Add ¾ cup sugar and bring to boil. Mix gelatin mixture with pineapple mixture, after taking it off the stove. Cool. Then add ½ cup grated cheese, 1 cup cottage and 1 bottle Avoset. (Do not whip Avoset) Put in mold and refrigerate.

Vi-Lani Robertson

SIMPLE POTATO SALAD

5 lbs. potatoes, boiled   1 bunch parsley
12 hard boiled eggs   ½ cup Best Food mayonnaise

Boil potatoes and eggs. Let cool. Add finely chopped parsley. Mix with mayonnaise. Chill. Some canned milk may be added to keep it moist. Also pitted olives for color. If more is wanted, add grated carrots.

Onion may be added minced. This does hasten the spoilage time. Serves 8-10.

Henry Piltz Kramer

PASTA SALAD

Cook 2 cups small pasta shells in boiling water with 1 pkg. frozen baby peas. Rinse and drain. While it cools and drains, chop ½ to 1 cup of each: celery, onion, green and red pepper.

Mince 1 clove garlic fine. Open and drain 1 can of tuna.

Toss all with mayonnaise to moisten well. Add a little sweet pickle relish to taste. Add any seeds and Italian seasonings, basil, oregano, salt and pepper, also to taste. Refrigerate for 2-3 hours.

Deborah Mullen

BANANA AND NUT SALAD

3 lge. or 6 small ripe bananas   ¾ cup mayonnaise
¼ cup lemon juice   ⅓ cup chopped nuts

Peel and cut bananas in halves lengthwise. Roll them in lemon juice, then in nuts. Place on lettuce leaves. Pour mayonnaise over them and serve.

Serves 6.

Julia Toomey

JELLO-COTTAGE CHEESE SALAD

1 20 oz. can crushed pineapple
1 16 oz. size cottage cheese
1 8 oz. Cool Whip
1 pkg. lime jello

Drain pineapple. Mix cottage cheese with Cool Whip; add pineapple. Sprinkle Jello powder over and mix well. Refrigerate a few hours before serving. Serves 4-6.

Sally McClellan

SAUERKRAUT SALAD

1 large can sauerkraut
1½ cups chopped green pepper

1 small jar chopped pimiento
1½ cups chopped onion

Mix all ingredients together in large bowl. Pour 1½ cups sugar on top. Do not stir. Refrigerate overnight. Mix and drain. Keeps well. Serves 8-10.

Jean St. John

BLACK CHERRY SALAD

1 size 2½ oz can pitted
   black bing cherries
1 cup grapefruit
¾ cup Port wine

1 3 oz. jar stuffed olives
½ cup lemon juice
2 pkgs. orange jello
¾ cup chopped pecan meats

Drain cherries. Take 1 cup cherry juice, lemon juice and enough water to make 1¾ cups liquid; heat, pour over jello and dissolve. Chill until partially set. Add cherries, grapefruit, nuts and olives. Add port wine. Unmold when firm and serve with mayonnaise on lettuce.

Erla Pauole

STEAMED TURKEY SALAD

About 1 lb. turkey breast fillet or boneless chicken breast,
   with skin removed
Dash of Schilling "Fine Herbs"
Dash of pepper
1½-2 tbsp. lemon juice

Place turkey in steamer. Sprinkle with other ingredients. Steam 15-20 minutes until done.

While meat is cooking prepare salad in large bowl. Suggested ingredients,

Lettuce	Mushrooms
Tomato	Avocado
Onion	Sliced zucchini
Green bell pepper	Grated carrot
Celery	Bean sprouts
Hard boiled egg	Croutons

When meat is cooked, dice into 1-1½ inch cubes and toss into salad. Serve with dressing of choice.

Zita Cup Choy

CHICKEN LONG RICE SALAD

1 bundle long rice	1 can chopped chicken
Juice of 1 lime	½ cup Chinese parsley

Soak long rice in water to soften. Boil long rice, al dente. Do not overcook. Rinse in cold water. Mix chicken in by hand. Pour lime juice over mixture. Sprinkle parsley on top. Refrigerate for one hour before serving.

Stuart W.H. Ching

SEA WEED SALAD

Mix lettuce with tomatoes. Add sea weed (limu).

Julia Toomey

OVERNIGHT SALAD

1 head lettuce
½ cup chopped onion greens
1 8 oz. can water chestnuts
1 10 oz. pkg. frozen peas
  - thaw only

1 tomato - remove seeds, slice
  meat of tomato into tidbits
1 cup grated mozzarella cheese
2 cups sliced mushrooms
1 cup celery, chopped

Soak off water and layer each item into 3 layers.

Dressing:
2 cups mayonnaise
¼ garlic clove,
  chopped or grated

2 tsp. white sugar

Mix together. Dilute with cream slightly to run slowly over salad.
Pour over salad and cool overnight.

Before serving sprinkle top with:
3 hard boiled eggs, chopped   Bacon bits

Serve directly from refrigerator.

Jeanne Read Alden

CURRIED CHICKEN SALAD

3 cups chicken, cubed
2 medium cucumbers

2 cups cantaloupe, cubed
½ cup slivered almonds, toasted

Dressing:
¼ cup mayonnaise
2 tbsp. chutney
½ tsp. curry powder
½ tsp. salt

⅛ tsp. nutmeg
⅛ tsp. pepper
1 cup yogurt

Mix dressing. Refrigerate dressing for 3 hours for flavors to blend.

Mix salad ingredients just before serving. Add dressing.

Salad may be served on lettuce or on cantaloupe slices. Serves 6.

Elizabeth Hammer

LIMU SALAD

There are several common limu (seaweed):

1. Lipoa
2. Lipeʻepeʻe
3. Aʻalaʻula
4. Limu Kohu
5. Huluhulu
6. Maneʻoneʻo

7. Limu ʻEleʻele
8. Manauea
9. Sea lettuce –
   Pahapaha and Pahaea
10. Kala

Be sure to clean your limu. Then cut/chop them.

Mix with lettuce or whatever green you wish for salad. For the dressing, use your own. Chill to cool then serve.

Julia Toomey

CRISPY DAY AHEAD SALAD

2 heads iceberg lettuce
1 10 oz. pkg. frozen peas
½ cup bacon chips
6 hard boiled eggs
2 cups shredded Swiss cheese

1 cup mayonnaise
1 tbsp. sugar
green onion garnish
salt and pepper

Layer the following:
In large bowl put:
    2 cups torn lettuce
    6 chopped hard boiled eggs
      (sprinkle with salt and pepper)
    Frozen peas
    Bacon chips
    Swiss cheese
    1 cup torn lettuce
    Salt and pepper

Over the top spread 1 cup mayonnaise evenly up to the sides of the bowl. This seals the salad underneath.

Sprinkle with sugar, salt and pepper. Garnish with green onion.

Refrigerate overnight. Serves 10.

June Bradley

HOT CHICKEN SALAD

4 hard boiled eggs
2 tbsp. lemon juice
1 tsp. salt
2 cups finely chopped celery
¾ cup cream of chicken soup
2 chopped pimientoes (optional)
4 cups chopped chicken
¾ cup mayonnaise
1 tbsp. chopped onion

Mix all ingredients and refrigerate overnight. Remove from refrigerator before baking. Cover with 1 cup crushed potato chips (and, if you like, 1 cup grated cheese). Bake at 400° for 25 or 30 minutes or until bubbly.

Mary Kirkham

HOT CHICKEN SALAD

This is a very tasty luncheon or soul-satisfying treat for a brunch. It can be prepared ahead and chilled overnight if desired and heated up quickly after guests arrive. It could also be made with left-over turkey. Good with French bread and fruit.

2 cups chicken, diced
2 cups celery, chopped
½ cup almonds, chopped
¼ tsp. salt
⅛ tsp. pepper
½ cup grated cheddar cheese
2 cups crushed potato chips
2 tsp. chopped onion or
1 tsp. inst. minced onion
2 tbsp. lemon juice
½ tsp. Accent
1 cup mayonnaise

Mix onion and lemon juice. Add remaining ingredients, except last 2. Mix well. Divide into 4 individual baking dishes or put into 9 in. pie pan. Mix chips and cheese and completely cover top of salad. Bake at 450° for 10 minutes.

David Lowman

PASTA SALAD WITH FAVA BEANS

Corkscrew noodles (pasta)
Ham
Canned corned beef
Tuna
Green and ripe olives
Young corn
Head and romaine lettuce
Chinese cabbage
Hard boiled eggs
Avocado
Fava beans (in a can at Safeway) Don't cook!
Petite peas

Boil the corkscrew noodles (pasta) for 12 minutes. Drain in colander. Add a bottle of Italian dressing. Add seasoning, pepper, oregano, basil, grated onions. Toss all together. Then layer everything.

First layer: Lettuce
Second layer: Chinese cabbage
Third layer: Pasta
Fourth layer: Frozen petite peas, uncooked

Continue with rest of ingredients.

Top with Fava and boiled eggs. Add layer of avocado last.

Ellen Vasconcellos

BANANA WALDORF SALAD

1½ cups diced ripe bananas   ⅓ cup chopped nuts
1½ cups diced apple   1 cup diced celery
¾ cup cooked salad dressing or
   mayonnaise

Have ingredients chilled before dicing. Combine with nuts and mayonnaise and serve on lettuce leaves. Garnish with pimiento strips or guava jelly. Serve it immediately. Serves 6.

Julia Toomey

7 UP SALAD

2 small cans crushed pineapple   1 cup chopped pecans
2 sm. pkgs. lime jello   or walnuts
2 sm. bottles 7 Up   2 cups boiling water
2 tsp. sugar   2 tsp. vanilla
2 8 oz. containers
   cream cheese, softened

Dissolve gelatin in hot water. Add the softened cream cheese to the hot water mixture and beat until smooth. The blender is fine for this. Fold in all the other ingredients and pour into slightly oiled molds. Chill until very firm. This makes a large salad – use a bundt pan.

Topping:
1 cup pineapple juice   ½ cup sugar
2 tbsp. flour   1 egg
1 cup Cool Whip

Mix pineapple juice, flour, sugar and egg (well beaten). Cook until thick. Let cool. Fold in the Cool Whip. Pour in center of salad mold. Re-chill.

Vi-Lani Robertson

Iolani Palace.

Breakfast in Honor of Rear-Admiral S. H. Upshur, U.S.N.

MAY 11th, 1885.

Musical Programme.

MARCH . . . . "KULA HIMENI." . . . . Berger

OVERTURE . . . . "FESTIVAL." . . . . Bach

GAVOTTE . . . . "WELCOME," . . . . Kluss

MEDLEY . . . . "YE OLDEN TIMES." . . . . Beyer

WALTZ . . . . "WAIMANALO," . . . . Berger

SELECTION . . . . "BELLS OF CORNEVILLE," . . . . Planquette

"STAR SPANGLED BANNER."

"HAWAII PONOI."

NOTES

BEEF AND BROCCOLI

½ lb. sirloin tip steak, slice thin   Oyster sauce
1 lb. bunch of broccoli   2 small cloves of garlic

Cut broccoli slating stems (thin). Cut flowerettes. Crush garlic and skin. Trim meat and slice diagonally. Marinate in refrigerator for at least ½ hour in:

½ tsp. baking soda   1 tsp. oyster sauce
1 tsp. soy sauce   1 capful rice wine
dash Ajinomoto   1 tsp. regular oil

Cook garlic in 2 tbsp. oil and discard. Brown and cook beef, add a little water. Remove beef. Start 2 tbsp. oil and stir fry broccoli. Add dash salt and ½ cup water. Cover and cook 5 minutes. Add meat and mix. Season with, mixed together:

1 tsp. soy sauce   ½ tsp. sesame oil
½ tsp. sugar   1 capful wine
Ajinomoto – dash   salt
2 tbsp. oyster sauce

Mix all ingredients well and push to one side. Have gravy mix ready (1 tsp. cornstarch to 3 tbsp. water). Add gravy mix to sauce in wok and stir well. Add more oyster sauce before serving. Serves 2-4.

Mary Nickel

SWEET-SOUR SPARE RIBS

Garlic, ginger and oil.

Fry spare ribs in above ingredients. Remove excess oil.

Simmer in: (until cooked)

⅓ cup apple cider vinegar. Add shoyu to make ¾ cup total.
1 cup brown sugar   Ajinomoto

You may thicken sauce before serving.

Pat Trask

MEXICAN POT ROAST

1 chuck roast
1 envelope onion soup mix
1 cup dry red wine

Bake roast until well done and falling apart. Drain roast. Save juice. When grease rises and become solid, remove. Shred meat and add to juice. Add the following ingredients:
1 15 oz. can garbanzo beans
1 15 oz. can rancho style beans
1 15 oz. can kidney beans
1 25 oz. can pinto beans
1 30 oz. can chile with beans
1 30 oz. can tamales
1 10 oz. can red enchilada sauce
1 10 oz. can green chili sauce

Flodie VanOrden

PEPPER STEAK

2 lbs. round steak
¼ tsp. pepper
½ cup flour
1 lge. onion, chopped
1 med. green pepper, sliced
1 cup mushroom pieces
1 can tomato soup
½ tsp. salt
¼ tsp. garlic salt
1 tbsp taco sauce
½ cup water

Cut round steak into serving pieces. Coat each piece in mixture of flour, salt, pepper and garlic salt. Brown pieces quickly in skillet in 1 tbsp. oil.

Place browned meat in casserole dish. Add onions, green peppers and mushrooms to skillet. Stir gently and cook about 5 min. Remove from heat. Combine tomato soup, water and taco sauce. Stir mixture and pour over meat pieces. Cover and bake at 350° for about 2 hrs. Serve over rice. 4-6 servings.

Josef Schlegel

BARBEQUED LAMB

6-7 lb. leg of lamb, butterflied
1 lge. garlic clove split
1-2 garlic cloves,
  according to taste
1½ tsp. salt
½ tsp. ground ginger
2 tbsp. chutney
⅔ cups salad oil
1 tsp. curry powder
¼ tsp. black pepper
⅓ cup lemon juice
1 cup white wine (optional)

Rub meat with garlic. Mix salt, curry, ginger and pepper. Rub lamb with mixture. Place in non-metallic dish. Chop chutney and garlic. Add juice, oil, wine. Pour over lamb and marinate several hours, preferably overnight.

To charcoal broil: Place lamb skin side up over medium fire 8 to 10 inches from heat. Baste and cook 25-30 minutes. Turn and cook 20-30 minutes.

Margaret Montgomery

LU'AU RIBS

3 lbs. spareribs (country style),
  cut in pieces
1 tsp. salt
Dash of pepper

Rub meaty spareribs on both sides with salt and pepper. Place ribs, meat side up in foil-lined shallow pan. Bake at 450° for 15 minutes. Drain off fat. Pour sauce over ribs. Bake at 350° for 1½ hours until tender, basting occasionally.

Sauce:

1 cup strained peaches
  (2 jars 4½ oz. baby food)
½ cup catsup
½ cup vinegar
⅔ cup brown sugar
2 tsp. ginger, grated
4 tbsp. shoyu
2 cloves garlic, minced

Mae Barth

MY DAD'S STEW

In one large stew pan you dump the following:

1 can corned beef	1 lge. chopped onion
2 medium diced potatoes	1 pkg. frozen green peas
1 lge. can tomatoes with juice	

Open your refrigerator – add any leftover dabs of corn, cabbage, green beans or green pepper. Rinse out any catsup bottles or small amounts of gravy. Be creative.

Cook over medium heat until potatoes and onions are tender. Test for addition of salt and pepper.

This serves at least 2 and depending on your leftovers – up to 5 hungry people – and it never is exactly the same twice!

Claire Hiett Gregorcyk

BARBARA'S HAWAIIAN STEW

5 lbs. stew meat	1 lge. onion
6 lge. ripe tomatoes	4 medium potatoes
1 medium carrot	2 stalks celery
1½ tbsp. Hawaiian salt	Cooking oil

In a big pot saute onion, cubed, in oil. Brown stew meat well and add water to cover meat. Cut tomatoes into chunks and add to meat. Bring to boil then let simmer for 1 hour. When meat is tender add potatoes, carrots and celery that have been cut into bite size pieces. When vegetables are soft add 1½ tbsp. Hawaiian salt or to taste.

Feeds 4-6 depending on who is eating it (Hawaiians) and with what (poi).

Barbara Pualani Lake

BEEF STEW

2-3 lbs. stewing beef (I prefer brisket)
3 cloves garlic, diced
1 tsp. salt (Hawaiian better)
¾ to 1 tsp. pepper
1 med. round onion, sliced
1 lge. stalk celery, chopped
1 bay leaf
1 6 oz. can tomato paste
3-4 med. potatoes (baking or russet)
2 lge. carrots

Brown meat with garlic, salt and pepper. Half way through add onion, celery and bay leaf and continue browning until the onion is translucent. Add the tomato paste and water to cover the meat. After the liquid boils, lower heat and simmer for about 1 hour periodically checking and adding water to retain liquid level. Add potatoes and carrots (cut into stew chunks) and continue cooking until the meat is tender and carrots are done. Serves 4.

Eloise Naone

BEEF TOMATO

1 lb. flank steak, sliced thin. Soak in marinade 15 minutes. Marinade:
3 tbsp. shoyu   1 tbsp. sherry
½ tsp. sugar   1 tbsp. cornstarch

1 piece ginger, crushed
1 clove garlic, crushed
1 med. onion
1 green pepper
2 stalks celery
2-3 tomatoes, cut in wedges
2 stalks green onion
Salt and pepper

Brown garlic, ginger in oil. Add beef – stir fry quickly. Remove from pan. Stir fry vegetables. Add beef and 1 cup water. Thicken with cornstarch. Serves 4-6.

Bernice Valenzona

CRISPY PORK

1 lb. lean pork	1 cup flour
2 tbsp. shoyu	Pinch of salt
1 tbsp. sugar	1 egg, ¼ cup water
1 clove star anise	Oil for frying
1 tbsp. sherry	2 cups water

Cut pork into 1 inch cubes. Put in sauce pan with 2 cups water, shoyu, sugar, anise, sherry. Simmer 45 minutes. Drain well.

Sift flour and salt. Make a well in center, drop in egg. Add water and stir into batter. Add pork pieces and coat. Deep fry in oil until crisp and golden. Drain. Serves 4-6.

Bernice Valenzona

QUICKY-BEEFY STROGANOFF

1 lb. round steak cut in ¾ inch cubes	1 10½ oz. can condensed tomato soup
Flour	1 tbsp. Worchestershire sauce
½ cup chopped onion	½ tsp. salt, dash of pepper
1 6 oz. can mushrooms, drained, save liquid	6-8 drops Tabasco
1 cup sour cream	2 tbsp. fat
	1 clove minced garlic

Dip meat in flour and brown in fat. Add onion, garlic and mushrooms. Combine sour cream, tomato soup, mushroom liquid and seasonings. Add to meat and simmer until tender, about 1 hour. Serve over rice or spaghetti. Serves 4-6.

Erla Pauole

BAKED SHORT RIBS

5 lbs. short ribs

2 cups sliced onions

Mix together:
¾ cups ketchup
2 tbsp. vinegar
2 tbsp. Worcestershire sauce

½ cup sugar
¾ cups water
4 tbsp. soy sauce

Place ribs in baking dish and scatter sliced onions over meat. Salt and pepper to taste. Put sauce mixture over meat and onions. Bake at 350° until done. Excellent using chuck roast, also.

Eleanor Azevedo

SWEET AND SOUR MEATBALLS

1 lb. lean ground beef
1 egg, beaten
1 med. clove garlic, crushed
1 tsp. salt
1 8 oz. can pineapple chunks
    in juice, undrained
1¼ cups sliced carrots
¾ cups sliced celery
2 tbsp. cider vinegar

1 tbsp. cornstarch
3 tbsp. A-1 steak sauce
½ cup soft bread crumbs
1 tbsp. oil
½ cup beef broth
¼ tsp. ground ginger
1 green pepper, cut in pieces

Combine beef, 3 tbsp. steak sauce, egg, bread crumbs, garlic, and salt. Form into 24 meatballs. In large skillet, brown meatballs well in oil. Drain. Add remaining ingredients, except cornstarch and green pepper. Cover and simmer 5 minutes. Dissolve cornstarch in water. Stir into mixture. Add green pepper. Simmer, uncovered for 5 minutes. Serve over rice. 4-6 servings.

Barbara Theus

LAMB SHISH KABOBS

2 lbs. lamb, boneless, cut into 1½ inch cubes
Water chestnuts   Cherry tomatoes
Mushrooms   Maui onion

Marinate lamb for 2 hours or overnight in:

½ cup wine vinegar   1 clove garlic, crushed
1 tsp. salt   ¼ tsp. pepper
½ tsp. oregano   ¼ tsp. paprika
½ cup salad oil

Skewer meat. Roast over hot coals separate from vegetables as vegetables cook rapidly. Serves 4.

Rosemary Eberhardt

SPARERIBS HAWAIIAN STYLE

2 sides lean spareribs   3 tbsp. brown sugar
2 tbsp. cornstarch   1 tbsp. shoyu
½ tsp. salt   ¼ cup vinegar
½ cup catsup   1 9 oz. can crushed pineapple

Cut ribs into serving size pieces. Combine sugar, cornstarch and salt in saucepan. Add vinegar, catsup, undrained pineapple and shoyu and bring to a boil, stirring constantly. Cook until slightly thickened.

Arrange ribs in oven proof dish and spoon sauce over so each rib is covered. Cover and bake at 350° for about 2 hours. Skim off excess grease and serve.

Barbara Theus

GREEN PEPPER STEAK

1 lb. beef chuck or round,
   fat trimmed
¼ cup soy sauce
1½ tsp. grated fresh ginger or
   ½ tsp. ground
¼ cup salad oil
1 cup red or green peppers
   cut into 1 inch squares

2 stalks celery, sliced
1 cup water
1 clove garlic
1 cup green onion, sliced
1 tbsp. cornstarch
2 tomatoes, cut in wedges

With a very sharp knife cut beef across grain into thin strips, ⅛ inch thick. Combine soy sauce, garlic, ginger. Add beef. Toss and set aside while preparing vegetables.

Heat oil in large frying pan or wok. Add beef and toss over high heat until browned. Taste meat. If it is not tender, cover and simmer for 30 to 40 minutes over low heat. Turn heat up and add vegetables. Toss until vegetables are tender crisp, about 10 minutes.

Mix cornstarch with water. Add to pan, stir and cook until thickened. Add tomatoes and heat through.

Serves 4.

Freida Theus

OVEN HAWAIIAN KALUA PIG

1 8 lb. pork loin roast
Seasoned salt

6 or 7 ti or banana leaves
Liquid smoke

Wash pork and rub with salt. Sprinkle a liberal amount of liquid smoke over the meat and wrap with ti or banana leaves and tie with a string. Wrap again in heavy foil and seal securely. Bake at 250° for 7 hours. Will serve a medium size family.

Barbara Theus

JIFFY LAU LAU DINNER

2 pkgs. Keoki's Lau Laus, 3 lau lau per package
(Chicken or pork)

Remove the ti leaves. Arrange the 6 lau laus in an oven proof dish or pan. Slightly chop, single layer. Sprinkle fresh grated coconut on top. Cover with foil and bake in oven at 300° for 25 minutes.

Microwave - cover with microwave plastic wrap and bake at Medium for 6 minutes. Serves 6.

June Bradley

CONTINENTAL VEAL

1½ lbs. veal steak
   1½ inches thick
1 egg beaten with 1 tbsp. water
1 onion sliced
¼ cup Crisco
1 cup milk

1 pkg. noodles
Salt and pepper to taste
bread crumbs
1 tsp. paprika
1 cup sour cream
½ cup slivered almonds

Cut veal into pieces for serving. Dip in crumbs then in beaten egg and again in crumbs. Cook onion slowly in melted Crisco until yellow. Remove onion from skillet. Brown veal quickly on both sides.

Reduce heat, add salt and pepper, paprika and onions.

Pour milk and sour cream over veal. Cover tightly and cook very slowly for 1 hour. Arrange veal on platter and surround with buttered cooked noodles. Sprinkle almonds over noodles. (All milk or all sour cream may be used if desired.) Serves 6.

Olive Linde

HAM BALLS

1½ lbs. ground ham	1 cup milk
½ lb. ground beef	1 lb. ground pork
1½ cups crushed graham crackers	2 eggs, beaten 1 onion, chopped

Form into large balls and bake 1 hour at 350°.

Make a sauce of:

2 cups tomato soup	¾ cup vinegar
2 cups brown sugar	2 tsp. dry mustard

Bring to a boil and pour over ham balls for last few minutes of baking time.

Mary Kirkham

STUFFED VEAL WITH SHRIMP

2 lbs. veal, thaw if frozen
1 cup chopped shrimp, thaw if frozen
1 sm. clove garlic, minced
½ tsp. dried rosemary, crushed (use rolling pin)
½ tsp. ground coriander
2 shallots, finely chopped
2 cups Almanden mountain sauterne
1 cup sour cream

Cut veal into 14 even pieces and pound each to ½ thickness. Sprinkle with salt and pepper.

Combine rest of ingredients except wine. Mix thoroughly. Top each veal slice, roll veal around filling and fasten with toothpicks. Heat 3 tbsp. clarified butter over medium heat. Brown stuffed veal quickly, adding more butter if needed. Add wine and simmer for 1 hour, turning once. Remove to hot serving dish. To remaining liquid in pan add 1 cup sour cream, stir until bubbly. Pour over stuffed veal and serve with hot noodles, rice or potatoes.

Belle Rogers

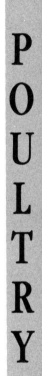

CHICKEN AND SNOW PEAS

3 lge. chicken breasts, split
  or cut into lge. pieces
⅓ cup flour
¾ cup chopped onion
1 clove garlic
1 can cream of mushroom soup
¼ cup dry sherry
¼ cup hot salad oil
½ cup sliced celery
Salt and pepper
1 cup sauteed fresh or
1 6 oz. can mushrooms

1 8 oz. can water chestnuts, drained and sliced
1 6 oz. pkg. snow peas, thawed or 2 cups fresh

Dredge chicken in flour. Salt and pepper it. Brown in hot oil. Drain, reserve drippings.

Saute onion, celery and garlic in drippings until tender.

Combine soup and sherry. Add soup mixture, mushrooms and water chestnuts to pan. Bring to a boil.

Return chicken to pan. Cover and simmer for 20 minutes. Add snow peas. Cover and simmer 10 minutes. Serve with rice.

Jackie March

BARBARA'S TERIYAKI CHICKEN

Delicious hot or cold

2-3 lbs. frozen chicken legs, thawed
½ cup soy sauce
½ cup sugar
¼ cup catsup
2 tbsp. sherry wine
1 tbsp. grated ginger
3 cloves garlic, minced
1 tbsp. sesame oil

Mix well. Marinate chicken in sauce 4-5 hours or overnight. Bake in 16x12x2 inch pan at 350° for 1 hour. Serves 4 to 5.

Luana McKenney

CHICKEN AND SOUR CREAM ENCHILADAS

1 lb. boneless and skinned chicken breasts, cubed
3 cans condensed cream of chicken soup
1 pt. sour cream
2 4 oz. cans diced green chilis
3 cups shredded Cheddar cheese
½ bunch green onions, chopped (⅓ cup)
1 pkg. flour tortillas (18)
Vegetable oil

Combine diced chicken, soup, sour cream and chilis in saucepan. Bring to a boil, stirring constantly. Reduce heat and simmer for 5 min. Heat oil in small saucepan and heat tortillas until flexible. Remove and drain on absorbent paper. Place 2 heaping tbsp. of chicken mixture on tortilla, roll and place in large baking pan. Pour remaining chicken mixture over tortillas, sprinkle with cheese and top with green onions. Bake in 350° oven uncovered about 30 minutes. Serves 8.

Preparation: 35 minutes   Cooking: 30 minutes

A crowd pleaser, easy and can be done ahead.
Easily doubled or tripled.

Roy McArdle

MOCHIKO CHICKEN

3 lbs. chicken, deboned and cut in pieces. Chicken thighs are good.

Soak in following mixture at least 5 hrs. or overnight, then fry.

4 tbsp. ea. of mochiko,   ¼ cup chopped green onions
   cornstarch and sugar   2 cloves garlic, minced
5 tbsp. shoyu   ½ tsp. salt and ajinomoto
2 beaten eggs

Pat Trask

ROAST CHICKEN WITH CHUTNEY DRESSING

¼ cup finely chopped dried apricots
¼ cup water   ½ lb. pork hash
1 cup finely chopped celery
½ cup finely chopped onion
¼ cup butter or margarine
¾ cup finely chopped water chestnuts
2 cups cooked rice   ¼ cup chutney
2 tbsp. parsley flakes
½ tsp. salt   ⅛ tsp. pepper
½ tsp. dried thyme leaves, crumbled
½ tsp. dried marjoram leaves, crumbled
½ tsp. poultry seasoning
1 fryer chicken (2½-3½ lbs.)
1 tsp. salt   2 tbsp. butter

Soak apricots in water overnight, drain. Cook and stir #1-6 ingredients with pork hash for 2-3 minutes. Add to cooked rice and mix
well. Heat oven to 375°. Rub 1 tsp. salt and garlic powder to chicken
cavity. Stuff cavity with rice stuffing. Fold wings across back with
tips touching. Brush chicken with melted butter. Place breast side
up in roasting pan. Baste occasionally with melted butter. Bake for
2¼-2½ hrs. Serve with chutney as condiment. Serves 6.

Vi-Lani Robertson

CHICKEN-CASHEW NUT-BAMBOO SHOOT –
PEKING STYLE

2 lbs. boneless chicken cut in bite size pieces
1 can bamboo shoots, sliced thin in 2 inch strips
1 can button mushrooms, sliced thin
5 cloves garlic, chopped fine
1-2 tsp. yakitori sauce
½ c. chopped cashew nuts
Cornstarch to thicken gravy
Sugar, salt and pepper to taste

Marinate chicken with garlic and yakitori sauce for 1 hr. Fry chicken
in oil. Do not overcook. Add bamboo shoots, sliced mushrooms.
Add cornstarch to thicken gravy. Top with cashew nuts. Serves 4
with rice.

Sally McClellan

PAPRIKAS CSIRKE – CHICKEN PAPRIKA

2 broiler-fryer chickens (about 3 lbs. each), cut into quarters
Salt, freshly ground black pepper

4 tbsp. butter

2 cups chopped onion

2 tbsp. flour

3 tbsp. sweet Hungarian paprika

2 cups rich homemade or
   canned chicken broth

2 cups sour cream

2 tbsp. vegetable oil

2 cloves garlic, chopped

4 tbsp. tomato paste

Rinse chicken with cold running water and pat dry with paper towels. Sprinkle with salt and pepper. Saute chicken in butter and oil in 12 in. skillet over medium heat until golden, 6 to 8 min. on each side. Remove chicken from skillet and drain off all but 1 tbsp. of fat.

Saute onion and garlic in fat over medium heat until light brown, about 6 minutes. Stir in flour, tomato paste and paprika until onion is evenly coated; then stir in broth. Return chicken to skillet and reduce heat to low. Simmer, covered, until chicken is done, 30 to 35 minutes, turning chicken once halfway through cooking.

Remove chicken from skillet and keep warm. Boil liquid in pan, stirring constantly, until slightly reduced and thickened, about 5 minutes. Stir in sour cream over low heat. Return chicken to skillet, and heat just till chicken is hot, 3 to 5 minutes.

Transfer chicken to heated serving platter. Spoon sauce over chicken; sprinkle with parsley. Garnish with tomato-peel "roses" and celery leaves. Serve immediately. Serves 8.

Josef Schlegel

HERB CHICKEN

3 to 4 lbs. chicken parts,
  skinned
½ tbsp. tarragon
½ tbsp. thyme
1 tbsp. seasoned salt
1 lge. lemon, sliced

1 tsp. freshly ground pepper
½ tbsp. basil
½ tbsp. garlic salt
3 tbsp. olive oil
juice of 1 lemon

1. Combine all seasonings and sprinkle over the chicken pieces.
2. Cover a baking dish with oil. Add the chicken and cover with
   lemon slices. Drizzle lemon juice over the chicken.
3. Bake at 350° for 30 minutes.
4. Turn the chicken and bake for 20 to 30 minutes longer.
5. Serve hot or cold. Remove lemon slices before refrigerating.

Serves 6.

Beverly Hansen

HERB CHICKEN

1 cup herb stuffing
1 chicken, cut up
¼ cup chopped parsley

½ cup melted butter
⅔ cups Parmesan cheese, grated
1 clove garlic, minced

Combine all dry ingredients. Dip chicken in melted butter and roll
in dry mixture. Place chicken in a shallow pan, skin side up. Sprinkle
with remaining butter and dry mixture. Bake for 45 minutes at 375°.

Erla Pauole

58

HONEY-CURRIED CHICKEN

5 lbs. chicken pieces –
   thighs or breasts
1 cup honey

4 tsp. curry powder
½ cup prepared mustard

Place chicken pieces in single layer in 9x13 inch baking dish. Mix all ingredients and pour sauce evenly over chicken. Bake at 350° for 1 hour or until done, turning pieces over several times. Serve with rice.

Mary Nickel

CHICKEN PAPRIKA

1 3 lb. Grade A chicken, cut up
¼ cup butter or margarine
2 tbsp. paprika
2 med. onions, thinly sliced
½ cup fresh mushrooms, sliced
1 cup whipping cream
Salt and pepper to taste

Heat butter or margarine in large skillet. Place chicken skin side down in skillet and cook about 15 minutes or until brown. Turn chicken and sprinkle with salt, pepper and paprika. Add onions and mushrooms. Cover and cook for 30 minutes or until chicken is done. Remove chicken and keep warm. Spoon any excess fat from skillet. Add cream to skillet and bring to boil while stirring. Pour sauce over chicken. Serves 4.

Josef Schlegel

BAKED CHICKEN

1 3 lb. frying chicken; cut up   1 can beef consomme
Flour   Salt and pepper to taste
3 cloves garlic, minced   3 tbsp. shoyu

Wash chicken pieces and gently pat dry. Coat chicken with flour seasoned with salt and pepper. Lay chicken pieces in 9x13 pan. Sprinkle minced garlic and shoyu over chicken. Pour beef consomme over chicken. Bake in 350° oven for 1½ hours, or until chicken is done.

Eleanor Azevedo

CHICKEN MOZZARELLA

1 tbsp. vegetable oil   ¾ cup shredded
⅔ cup Bisquick   mozzarella cheese
2 tsp. Italian seasoning   2 tbsp. grated Parmesan cheese
¼ tsp. pepper   ¾ tsp. paprika
6 lge. chicken breast halves   ¾ cup chili sauce

Brush bottom of 9x13 pan with oil. Mix Parmesan cheese, Bisquick, Italian seasoning, paprika and pepper. Coat chicken. Arrange chicken, skin sides down in pan.

Bake 45 minutes at 425°. Turn chicken. Divide chili sauce among breast halves. Sprinkle with mozzarella cheese. Bake until melted, about 5 minutes. Sprinkle with parsley if desired. Serves 6.

Barbara Theus

EASY CHICKEN CORDON BLEU – HAWAIIAN STYLE

6 boned, skinned chicken breasts
6 thin slices ham
6 chunks, or slices, of Swiss cheese

Pound breast until thin and arrange in square shape. Place a slice of ham and a piece of cheese on each breast. Roll up and place, seam side down, close together in a shallow pan. Be sure ends of chicken cover the ends of the cheese.

Blend:
1 can mushroom soup   ½ can cream of chicken soup
¾ cup milk   1 chicken bouillon cube
⅛ cup cooking sherry

Pour over chicken. Top with small can crushed pineapple, drained well and 2 oz. chopped macadamia nuts.

Bake at 350° for 45 minutes. Do not overcook! Serves 6.

Mary Reed Hughes

CHICKEN WITH ORANGE SAUCE

2 chicken breasts, deboned   ½ cup chopped onion
2 tbsp. butter   ⅔ cup orange juice
1 tsp. grated orange peel   2 tsp. salt
⅓ cup dry sherry   1 medium bay leaf
2 tbsp. sugar
dash of pepper and
   garlic powder

Wash, sprinkle chicken breast with salt and garlic powder. Brown chicken on both sides in butter for 2 minutes. Remove chicken. In same skillet add chopped onion. Cook until tender. Add grated orange peel, orange juice, sherry, sugar, salt, pepper and bay leaf. Return chicken to pan and simmer for 20 minutes. Add orange sauce to thicken.

Orange Sauce: Combine 1 tbsp. cornstarch with 1 tbsp. cold water. Stir into gravy mixture. Bring to a boil. Cook and stir 1-2 minutes. Serve with seasoned rice. Serves 2-3.

Vi-Lani Robertson

NOTES

SEAFOOD

CLAM LINGUINE (creamy sauce)

1 cup fresh mushrooms
1 clove garlic minced
¼ cup minced onion
¼ cup margarine
3 tbsp. flour
2 cans (6½ oz. each) chopped clams, drained. (RESERVE LIQUID)
1 cup table cream
¼ cup Parmesan cheese, grated
1 tbsp. dry sherry or white wine
2 tbsp. chopped parsley
¼ tsp. pepper
Linguine, cooked

In medium saucepan, saute mushrooms, garlic and onion in margarine. Gradually stir in flour, clam liquid and cream. Cook until thickened. Add clams, cheese and seasonings. Heat thoroughly on low heat. Serve over hot linguine. Serves 6.

Optional: Add 1 dozen clams in shell that have been scrubbed and steamed – over the linguine and sauce.

Optional: Add to sauce ½ cup shredded carrots just prior to pouring on linguine – also extra chopped parsley.

Mary Helen Hooululahui Styan

SWEET AND SOUR FISH

Sauce:

1 tbsp. cornstarch	1 tbsp. shoyu
⅓ cup vinegar	2 tbsp. oil
⅓ cup water	1 toe ginger root
½ cup sugar	

Mix ingredients in a pot. Bring to a boil. Buil for 1½ minutes. Add shredded vegetables such as bell pepper, onions, carrots. Use as many as you wish.

Batter: 2 eggs, thickened with Bisquick and thinned with milk and water as needed.

Fish: Boneless, cut into 1½ inch squares. Dip in batter and deep fry until golden brown. Place on platter, pour sauce over and serve.

Ann Fagerroos

LOBSTER OR SHRIMP NEWBURG

3 frozen rock lobster tails or 1½ lb. shrimp	1 tsp. parsley or chopped chives
1 can shrimp soup	1 cup of milk
1 tbsp. chopped onion	2 tbsp. butter
2 tbsp. sherry	

Saute shrimp or lobster, onion, parsley in skillet on low heat for 3 minutes. Add shrimp soup, milk and flavoring. Bring to a boil, simmer for 5 minutes. Serve over hot rice. Serves 4.

Marge Stromgren

MAHIMAHI IN TI LEAVES

Needed: mahimahi fillets, deboned. Ti leaves, salt and pepper, paprika, butter, lemon juice and slivered almonds.

Place fish on ti leaves. Sprinkle with seasonings. Brush generously with butter and lemon juice. Fold up the ti leaves and tie with a string. Broil over charcoal 20 minutes or bake at 350° for 30 minutes.

Place the almonds in butter and brown in a skillet. Pour over fish.

Barbara Theus

SHRIMP A LA CREOLE

3 lbs. peeled shrimp
1 green pepper, chopped
⅓ cup oil
5 lge. stalks celery, chopped
Light sprinkle cayenne pepper

2 cups chopped onions
4 cloves garlic, minced
1 lge. can tomato paste
1 tbsp. sugar
2 8 oz. cans tomato sauce

Cook chopped ingredients in oil (low heat) about 20 minutes. Add tomato sauce and paste. Add 3 cups water, or a little more. Simmer about 30 minutes then add shrimp and simmer 30 minutes longer. Serve over cooked rice. Serves 8 or more.

Mae Barth

OPAKAPAKA (RED SNAPPER)

1-2 lb. fish, fillet
½ tomato (wedge)
6 pcs. fresh ginger
Pinch of black pepper
Pinch of salt (optional)
1 tsp. wine

½ round onion (wedge)
1 tsp. of parsley
1½ tbsp. mayonnaise
1 tsp. of oregano
1 tsp. lemon juice

Lay fish on foil. Spread mayonnaise on one side of fish. Add in order: Black pepper, oregano, parsley, ginger, onion, tomato, lemon juice, wine.

Wrap fish in foil. Steam for ½ hour to 45 minutes or bake at 350° 20-25 minutes. Serves 2.

Josephine Matthews

LORENZO'S ITALIAN STYLE AHI
(YELLOW FIN TUNA)

1 lb. ahi sliced into
   ¼ inch thick slices
3 onions sliced into rings

¼ tsp. salt
¼ cup red wine vinegar
¼ tsp. black pepper

Wash fish in cold water. Pat dry with paper towels. Heat oil in skillet. Brown ahi on both sides. Remove from skillet and place on serving dish. Add onions, salt and pepper and red wine. Cook until onion is translucent. Pour over cooked ahi. Serve at room temperature with garlic bread and vegetable. Serves 2-4.

Grace Parker

SQUID LU'AU

1 lb. squid
sugar to taste (optional)
1 16 oz. can frozen coconut milk

2 cups cooked lu'au leaves
¾ cup water

Cut the squid into 1 inch pieces and boil till tender. The outer skin may be removed. Leave a little water in the pan with the squid. Cook the lu'au leaves separately with a little water until they do not sting. Boil 1½ hrs. Change water and boil ½ hr. longer.

Add the cooked lu'au leaves to the squid. Bring to a boil for a few minutes and add to thawed coconut milk, simmer. Do not boil after adding the coconut milk. Serve immediately.

Barbara Theus
(from Eloise K. Carillo)

STEAMED MULLET – KOREAN STYLE

2 lb. fish
1 tsp. toasted sesame seeds
¼ tsp. garlic

4 tbsp. shoyu
¼ tsp. ginger

Brown fish on both sides. Add above sauce in belly and on the fish. Cover and allow to steam for 10 minutes with heat off. Serves 2-4.

Colleen Murakami

RED SNAPPER, VERACRUZ STYLE

2 lb. red snapper filets
2 cloves garlic, minced
1 lge. onion, chopped
About 3 tbsp. olive oil
3½ cups (#2½ can) canned tomatoes, chopped
1 sm. can pimiento, drained and coarsely chopped
⅓ cup lemon juice
2 tbsp. capers, rinsed and drained
½ cup pitted green olives, sliced
2 tbsp. finely chopped parsley
2 tsp. dried oregano
Salt and freshly ground pepper

1. Wilt the onion and garlic in hot oil.
2. Add tomatoes, lemon juice, oregano, salt and pepper. Cook about 5 minutes to blend the flavors.
3. Place the filets in a buttered baking dish. Sprinkle with pimientos, capers, olives and parsley. Pour the tomato sauce over.
4. Cover baking dish with foil. Bake 25 to 30 minutes at 350° or until the fish flakes easily with a fork.

Serves 5

Beverly Hansen

HALPRIKAS – Fish Paprika

1½ lbs. fresh white fish
3 large onions
2 tsp. sweet paprika

1½ lbs. fresh blue fish
1 green pepper

Cut fish into slices 1½ inches thick. Soak in salt water for 1 hour.

Mince 3 large onions and fry onions in 2 level tsp. fat. Add 2 tsp. of sweet paprika.

Place fish and other ingredients in a wide pan and add a few slices of green pepper.

Pour enough water into pan to cover fish slices.

Boil 30 to 35 minutes without stirring. Remove fish slices from pan. Stir sauce and pour over fish.

Brian Miller

SEAFOOD DELIGHT – Pu Pu

1 can cream of mushroom soup
1 envelope Knox gelatin
¾ cup mayonnaise
1 cup minced celery

1 can crab, or shrimp, or
    clams (drain well)
3 tbsp. cold water
8 oz. cream cheese
1 small grated onion

Dissolve gelatin in cold water. Add to warm soup. Add other ingredients.

Rinse a mold with cold water. Pour in mixture and refrigerate overnight. Garnish with parsley. Serve with Ritz or Wheatsworth crackers, or with lavosh.

Rosemary Eberhardt

ROSE WILDER'S CRABMEAT

Melt 1 stick margarine (or butter) with ¼ lb. grated cheddar cheese. Stir in a few dash of Worcestershire sauce, 1 beaten egg yolk and 1 can crabmeat. Spread on buns or English muffins and broil until lightly browned and bubbly. 8 muffin halves.

Jean St. John

PINEAPPLE FISH

1 lb. mahimahi cut into bite size pieces

Batter:
1 cup flour	Pinch of salt
1 egg	½ cup water

Mix well together. Dip fish in batter and deep fry.

4 Pineapple rings cut up roughly. Add to fish.

Sauce:
2 tbsp. brown sugar	½ cup pineapple syrup
2 tbsp. vinegar	(from canned pineapple)
1 tsp. finely chopped	Salt to taste
fresh ginger	1 tbsp. cornstarch
	1 tbsp. shoyu

Bring to a boil. Boil 2-3 minutes. Pour over fish.

1 pkg. toasted almond pieces (fry in oil).
Sprinkle over fish. Serves 3-4

Bernice Valenzona

SPICED PICKLED SHRIMP

5 small white onions,	4 cloves garlic
thinly sliced	Salt
2 10 oz. pkgs. frozen shrimp	½ cup Italian olive oil
¼ cup vinegar	Bay leaves

Cut up onions. Boil shrimp. Layer shrimp and onions in bowl. Mix olive oil, vinegar, garlic, bay leaves and salt. Pour over shrimp. Refrigerate 24 hours. Cover. Stir frequently to blend flavors. Cool and serve the next day. Delicious! Serves 8.

Elizabeth Hammer

SALMON LOAF

Large can red salmon
2 tbsp. flour
1 cup milk
2 eggs

1 tsp. baking powder
2 tbsp. melted butter
Salt and pepper

Clean salmon, separate eggs. Mix milk, yolks of eggs, flour and baking powder. Add melted butter, salt and pepper. Beat egg whites and add last.

Bake in greased casserole in pan of water for ½ hour in 350° oven. Olive and/or mushrooms may be added. Serves 4.

Mae Barth

SHELLFISH STUFFED AHI (YELLOW FIN TUNA)

1 tbsp. margarine or butter
1 cup dried Maui onions
½ cup diced celery
4 oz. cooked shrimps

4 oz. cooked crab meat
¾ lb. Ahi filet ½ inch thick
Dash paprika on top
1 sm. clove garlic, minced

Preheat oven to 350°. Melt margarine in 9 inch skillet over medium high heat. Saute garlic, onion, celery, black pepper and salt for 1 minute. Add in cooked shrimps and crab meat. Saute for 1 minute.

Remove the skillet from heat. Spread the sauteed shellfish mixture evenly on the bottom of a 1 quart casserole. Cover the shellfish mixture with ahi filet. Spread the mayonnaise evenly on the ahi filet. Bake until done. Serves 2-3.

Kapulani Silva

Menu.

——

FRUIT.

——

FISH :

BOILED KUMU.   FRIED MULLET.

CRAB.

——

BROILED :

STEAK.   VEAL CUTLETS.

——

SALMI OF DUCK.   PIGEON.

——

SHRIMP CURRY.

——

SWEET OMELET.   ICE CREAM.

——

TEA.   COFFEE.

VEGETABLES

ROMAN PIE

2 cups elbow macaroni
10 oz. sharp cheddar cheese
1 cup salad olives (green)
1 green pepper

2 sm. cans mushrooms
  (optional)
2 cans tomato soup
1 onion
2 eggs (optional)

Cook macaroni. Steam or fry sliced onions, peppers and mushrooms at same time. Shred cheese. Boil eggs. Combine macaroni, soup, olives, onions and peppers.

When cool add cheese. Put in casserole in layers with sliced boiled eggs. Bake 1 hour at 350°.

Marge Stromgren

BROCCOLI PUFF

1 10 oz. pkg. frozen broccoli cuts
1 can condensed cream of mushroom soup
2 oz. (½ cup) sharp process American cheese, shredded
¼ cup milk   1 beaten egg
¼ cup mayonnaise   1 tbsp. butter, melted
¼ cup fine dry bread crumbs

Cook broccoli, omitting salt. Drain thoroughly. Place in 10x6x1½ inch baking dish.

Stir together soup and cheese. Gradually add milk, mayo and egg to soup mix. Stir until well blended. Pour over broccoli.

Combine bread crumbs with butter. Sprinkle evenly over soup mixture. Bake at 350° for 45 minutes.

Deborah Mullen

EGGPLANT FRITTERS – Armenian

2 Medium eggplants

1 onion

Pinch of salt and pepper

1 cup olive oil, or any fat oil

1 lb. chopped lamb

4 eggs

Chop onion in small pieces. Mix with chopped meat and add salt and pepper. Cook for about 15 minutes. Wash eggplant and cut in slices about ¼ inch thick. Spread meat mixture on slices of eggplant and cover with another slice of eggplant. Dip in beaten eggs and fry in oil.

Brian Miller

HOT CABBAGE SLAW

3 egg yolks

1 tsp. salt

¼ tsp. paprika

⅓ cup sugar

1 cup water

4 cups shredded cabbage

¼ cup chopped green pepper

2 tbsp. flour

½ tsp. dried mustard

¼ tsp. celery seed

⅓ cup vinegar

¼ cup cream

1 cup shredded apple

Beat egg yolks, add flour, salt, mustard, paprika, celery seed and sugar. Pour in vinegar and water. Cook slowly and stir constantly until the dressing thickens. Pour in remaining ingredients. Mix, pile in serving bowl.

Helen V. Rantala

STUFFED PATTYPAN SQUASH

6 pattypan squash	4 slices lean bacon
¼-½ cup minced onion	½ tsp. salt
Freshly ground pepper	½ tsp. basil
2 tbsp. minced parsley	½ cup white wine

1. Cut tops off the squash and carefully scoop out the centers, leaving a firm shell. A small melon ball cutter works well but it can also be done with the tip of a teaspoon.
2. Discard the seeds and coarsely chop the squash flesh, including the cut off top.
3. In a skillet, fry the bacon until crisp, then drain and crumble it.
4. Saute the onion in the remaining bacon fat until softened. Add the chopped squash and cook 2-3 minutes longer, stirring well.
5. Mix in the crumbled bacon, salt and pepper, basil and parsley. Spoon this mixture into the squash shells.
6. Arrange the pattypans in a shallow greased baking pan. Pour in dry white wine around them. Cover pan tightly with foil.
7. Bake until the squash is tender, about 30 minutes.

Serves 4-6

Beverly Hansen

SCALLOPED POTATOES

Rub the inside of a shallow gratin dish or cake pan with a cut garlic clove. Let the juice dry, then butter the dish generously. Peel potatoes and slice into ⅛ inch slices. Arrange the slices in the dish in rows, slightly overlapping both the slices and the rows. Salt each layer. Do not fill the dish more than ⅔ full.

Pour milk into the dish until the potatoes are about half-covered. Top the slices with a layer of cream deep enough to cover.

Put the uncovered dish in a pre-heated 400° oven. After 15 minutes reduce the heat to 350° and bake for a further 45 minutes until the potatoes have absorbed the milk and the cream has formed a golden crust over the surface.

Beverly Hansen

LUP CHONG AND BROCCOLI

1 lb. pkg. Lup Chong   1 large bunch of broccoli
¼ tsp. shoyu   ½ cup water

Clean broccoli. French cut both the lup chong and broccoli. Fry lightly. Add broccoli, shoyu and water in skillet and cover. Cook 3 to 4 minutes or until broccoli is cooked. Serves 7-8

Samuel Kaliko Sin Jui Ah Yuen, Jr.

STUFFED ZUCCHINI

3 medium zucchini   1 tsp. salt, optional
1 lb. ground browned turkey   1 tsp. lemon juice
2 tsp. dehydrated onion flakes ¼ tsp. pepper
2 tsp. parsley flakes   ⅔ cup spaghetti sauce
1 tsp. oregano flakes or powder ¼ cup mayonnaise

Cut zucchini in half lengthwise. Scoop out center leaving a ¼ inch shell.

Place on shallow baking dish.

Chop zucchini centers and mix with next 8 ingredients. Spoon mixture into shells and top with portions of spaghetti sauce.

Bake in 350° oven for 30 minutes. Serves 4.

Kapulani Silva

BAKED ZUCCHINI DISH

4 zucchini (Italian squash)
2 fresh tomatoes or 1 can of Italian style tomatoes
1 tbsp. parsley
1 sliced leek or 2 sliced green onions
¼ lb. Parmesan cheese
Salt and freshly ground pepper

1. Wash zucchini. Cut into ½ inch slice.
2. Peel fresh tomatoes. Whether using fresh or canned tomatoes, squeeze out the juice and seeds. Chop.
3. Layer zucchini, chopped tomatoes, parsley, leek or onion and cheese slices. Season.
4. Bake at 350° for about 30 minutes. Serves 4.

Beverly Hansen

CARBONARA WA'AHILA

1 lb. uncooked noodles
½ lb. grated Parmesan
6 egg yolks
¼ cup crumbled bacon
    (optional)

½ lb. butter
½ lb. grated romano cheese

Cook noodles in boiling water until al dente. Drain. Add butter to noodles. Toss lightly. Add cheese and mix thoroughly. Add egg yolks and crushed bacon.

For variation you may substitute a portion of the butter with bacon grease. Fettucine noodles are what is usually used, however you can be creative and use any type of noodle.

Variations: Cooked chopped broccoli, spinach, carrots, cauliflower may be added in any combination. Cooked shrimp, crab and lobster can also be added. If you do, I suggest deleting bacon.

Serves 4-6 as a main course.

Darryl Keola Cabacungan

SPAGHETTI NOODLES

1 lb. spaghetti,
   cooked and blanched
1 tbsp. Wesson oil
½ lb. sliced pork
½ cup water
1 stalk celery, sliced

3 cloves garlic, chopped fine
½ packet dashi no moto
½ tsp. Hawaiian salt
¼ tsp. pepper
½ round onion, sliced
1 med. carrot, julienned

Any 2 of the following: 6 string beans, julienned
   1 whole stem broccoli and flowers, sliced
   5 cauliflower sections, sliced
   ½ lb. Chinese peas

After spaghetti is drained, toss with 1 tbsp. Wesson oil, 1 tsp. sesame oil, 1 tbsp. oyster sauce and 1 tsp. shoyu. Let stand. Brown pork with oil, garlic, salt and pepper. Add ½ packet dashi and ½ cup water. Simmer until liquid dries. One by one gradually stir fry in onion, carrot, celery and 2 other kinds of vegetables, making sure vegetables remain crisp. Stir in spaghetti, season to taste with oyster sauce and shoyu. Garnish with sliced char siu and Chinese parsley. Serves 4

Eloise Naone

POTATOES BOULANGERE

Choose the size of pan you want. Peel potatoes – enough to fill pan. Slice potatoes lengthwise, cut each half to make half moons. Butter pan. Arrange in pan. Cover with chicken stock. Before adding stock chop 1 large onion and sprinkle over potatoes.

Brown in 350° oven for 1½ hours or until brown.

Variation: Tomato sauce

Kimberly Garner

ELABORATE ALI'I SPINACH

2 pkgs. frozen chopped spinach
3 lge. tomatoes
¼ cup bread crumbs
⅓ cup chopped onion
4 tbsp. melted butter or
   margarine

⅓ cup grated Parmesan
   cheese
¼ tsp. salt
½ tsp. garlic
2 eggs, beaten
½ tsp. crumbled thyme

Cook and drain spinach. Peel and slice tomatoes in 10-12 thick slices. Lay them flat in baking dish. Mix spinach with remaining ingredients. Spoon spinach mixture on top of tomatoes. Sprinkle with bread crumbs and cheese. Bake at 350° for 15 minutes.

Serves 8.

Suzie Anderson

RORY'S SPINACH QUICHE

2 pkgs. chopped spinach. Thaw, drain, cook only until heated through
6 beaten eggs
2 chopped Bermuda onions
6 tbsp. melted margarine
½ tsp. thyme

2 cups herb stuffing mix
¾ cup mozzarella cheese
1 tsp. garlic salt, or to taste
½ tsp. pepper

Mix. Chill. Place in 10 inch pie plate. Bake at 325° for 20 minutes or until firm. Accent: mustard sauce. Serves 6

Jeanne Read Alden

CORN STUFFED TOMATOES

6 firm medium tomatoes. Slice off tops and remove pulp. Save.
¼ cup butter or margarine
1½ tsp. garlic salt
2 tbsp. finely chopped onion
2 cups thinly sliced zucchini
   (optional or replace with
   added corn [1 more cup])

1 cup canned corn
½ tsp. dillweed
Swiss cheese

Saute onion, zucchini, garlic salt and dillweed until tender in melted margarine. Stir in flour, corn and tomato pulp. When slightly thickened fill tomato shells. Bake at 350° for 5-12 minutes. Top with grated Swiss cheese.

Jeanne Read Alden

OLD FASHIONED BAKED BEANS

2 cups dry beans	4 tbsp. sugar
6 cups water	½ tsp. dry mustard
1 tsp. salt	1 lge. onion, peeled
4 tbsp. molasses or karo	1 ham hock or salt pork

Pick over and wash beans. Add 6 cups water and soak beans overnight. The next day cook beans in same water over low heat for 1½ hrs. or until just tender.

Add remaining ingredients, except pork. Cut pork into small pieces. Add ½ pork to beans and place in casserole or bean pot.

Push onion into center of beans. Top with remaining pork. Cover and bake at 275° for 5-6 hrs.

If using ham hock, push it in before the onion.

Charlotte Clarke

BAKED BEAN DELIGHT

2 lge. cans cooked brown beans, drained

¾ cup brown sugar	½ sliced onion
1 tbsp. butter or oleo	¼ cup yellow mustard

Saute onions in butter or margarine until tender. Mix brown sugar in and add mustard. Stir until blended. Add all to brown beans, blend and place in Pyrex loaf dish. Bake at 350° for 30-40 minutes. Serves 8.

Jeanne Read Alden

HAM HOCKS AND BEANS

1 or 2 ham hocks	1 can tomato sauce
3 pcs. garlic, smashed fine	Salt and pepper
1 small onion, diced	1 pkg. dry kidney beans
1 tbsp. parsley or parsley flakes	Cut up potatoes

Boil ham hocks about 2 hrs. Cover meat with water. Add water as needed. Add beans, boil about 1-1½ hr. more. Add potatoes and rest of ingredients. Cook until potatoes are done. Add sliced Portuguese sausage if desired.

Barbara Theus

NOTES

SHRIMP, CHICKEN OR LAMB WITH COCONUT CURRY SAUCE

¼ lb. butter or margarine
½ cup flour
1 cup milk
2 cans unsweetened coconut milk
1 large onion finely chopped
2 tbsp. curry powder (adjust to taste)
Salt and Pepper to taste
1 stalk of lemon grass (optional)
3 cups cooked shelled, deveined shrimp, shredded chicken
        or cubed lamb.

Melt butter or margarine in large skillet or heavy pot. Add onion and cook until translucent. Stir in flour slowly to make a roux. Add curry powder. Slowly add milk, blending into roux. Add stalk of lemon grass whole (optional).

Cook on low heat, stirring constantly, until mixture becomes very thick. Slowly add coconut milk, stirring until consistency of thick cream sauce. Do not boil. If sauce does not thicken sufficiently, mix more flour in separate bowl with milk or water and add, stirring until sauce thickens. More curry powder may be added in the same way.

Remove lemon grass. Add shrimp, chicken or lamb.

Serve over hot rice with the following condiments on the side:

Chutney
Chopped hard cooked egg
Cooked chopped bacon
Chopped peanuts or macadamia nuts
Chopped green onion
Unsweetened shredded coconut
Raisins

Very nice accompanied by baked or fried bananas and green salad.

Serves about 8.

Alice F. Guild

AUNT LILLIAN'S SPAGHETTI (Old Family Recipe)

1 pkg. spaghetti
1 can tomato soup
1 lb. ground beef
Salt to taste

2 tbsp. Worcestershire sauce
1 cup canned corn
1 lge. onion
¼ cup butter

Cook spaghetti until tender. Melt butter in frying pan, add onion and meat. Cook until brown.

Mix all ingredients together. Put in baking dish. Sprinkle top with grated cheese and bake at 375° until brown.

Good with baking powder biscuits or corn bread.

Helen V. Rantala

FRUIT CURRY

1 large can peaches (the Country type if you can find them.)
1 large can pears
1 large can apricot halves
1 large can pitted plums or pitted prunes
1 large can pineapple sticks or cubes
½ cup raisins

Drain fruit. Make a sauce of:
1 stick butter or oleo
6 tsp. good curry powder

1 cup brown sugar

Heat together until butter is melted. Blend well. Pour sauce over fruits in casserole. Cook uncovered in 325° oven for 1 hour. Stir occasionally.

Serve warm. Excellent with baked ham, meat loaf, or fowl. Good for a buffet table, too.

Helen V. Rantala

SALT FREE VEGETABLE LASAGNE

8 oz. lasagne, cooked
1 lb. cottage cheese
8 oz. American cheese
½ tsp. garlic powder
1 lb. zucchini, spinach
   or cabbage

1 lb. spaghetti or pizza sauce
1 lb. mushrooms
8 oz. Mozzarella cheese
2 tbsp. butter or marg.

Grease well with the butter or margarine a 9x13 inch or 10x14 inch pan. Put layer of lasagne, layer of vegetables, cheeses, mushrooms. Start again till all ingredients are used, making last layer lasagne. Pour spaghetti or pizza sauce over and top generously with cheese.

Preheat oven 5 minutes. Bake at 375° for 40-45 minutes.

Serves 6 to 8 hungry people. With a green salad it makes a delicious meal.

The following can be substituted for the vegetables:

1 large onion chopped and sauted.
1 lb. of chopped meat, sauted. Discard some of the fat. Add the onions and spread over lasagne instead of vegetables.

Sophie Perrenoud

CORNED BEEF CHOP SUEY

½ round onion, sliced
1 can corned beef
1 pkg. fresh chop suey mix

Saute onion. Add chop suey mix. Cook 2 minutes. Form into a ring. Add crumbled corned beef to center. Cover and cook 4 more minutes. Serve with rice. Serves 2.

Sally McClellan

CRAB CASSEROLE

1 lb. crab meat	1 tbsp. melted butter
½ cup minced celery	¼ cup bread crumbs
2 tbsp. minced green pepper	2 tbsp. flour
¼ cup butter melted	1 egg yolk, beaten
1 cup milk	½ tsp. salt
2 tbsp. lemon juice	

1. Remove shell from crab meat.
2. Saute celery and green pepper in ¼ cup butter until softened.
3. Blend in flour and cook until the mixture bubbles well, stirring vigorously.
4. Carefully stir a little of the hot sauce into the beaten egg yolk. Add this egg sauce into the main sauce, stirring well.
5. Add lemon juice, seasonings and crab meat.
6. Pour into a buttered 1 qt. casserole.
7. Combine 1 tbsp. butter and crumbs. Sprinkle over the crab mixture.
8. Bake at 350° for 20 to 25 minutes or until lightly browned.

Serves 4

Beverly Hansen

BROCCOLI CASSEROLE

2 pkgs. chopped broccoli - cook 3 minutes in boiling water and drain well.

Mix together:

1 beaten egg	1 can sliced water chestnuts
1 cup mayonnaise	1 grated onion
1 can cream of mushroom soup	1 cup shredded cheese

Add to broccoli, mix and pour into a buttered casserole dish. Cover with cheese and cracker crumbs. Bake 25 minutes at 350°. Serves 6.

Mary Bennett

FOR PEOPLE WHO HATE TO COOK!

CHEESE CASSEROLE

1 pkg. frozen chopped broccoli
2 cups Minute rice
1 can cheddar cheese soup
1 small can chunk chicken

Prepare broccoli per microwave instructions.

Prepare Minute rice in medium pan on stove. When rice is done, add broccoli, soup and chicken. Blend and heat until warm. You may pour this into casserole dish and top with breadcrumbs or grated cheddar cheese and pop in oven for about 15 minutes to melt cheese. Serve with fruit salad and rolls.

Linda Norris

TAMALE CASSEROLE

2 cans of tamales
½ cup grated cheddar cheese
½ cup chopped onions
1 lge. can chili

Unwrap tamales and cut into about 3 pieces each. Place in 2 quart casserole dish. Top with chili and chopped onions. Bake at 350° for 30 minutes. Top with cheese and return to oven for 5-10 minutes until cheese is melted. Serve with warm flour tortillas instead of rolls for a little Mexican flare.

Linda Norris

SAUERKRAUT AND POLISH KIELBASA

Ingredients:

1 large onion	2 lb. sauerkraut
2 cloves garlic	2 lb. potatoes
2 tbsp. Wesson oil	1 lb. Kielbasa
3 tbsp. red wine	½ lb. piece of ham
1 lge. bay leaf	4 cloves or nutmeg

Preparation:

Saute chopped onion and garlic in oil. Rinse sauerkraut and add to onions. Saute for at least 15 minutes. Add bay leaf and cloves.

Peel potatoes, wash and cut each into 4 pieces. Cook in hot water until almost done. Add to sauerkraut. Add Kielbasa and ham. Cook 5 minutes.

Remove potatoes, Kielbasa and ham to separate plate. Cover. Now to the sauerkraut – add the red wine, mix and cook 2 more minutes. Serves 6.

Bon appetit!

Sophie Perrenoud

CRABMEAT AND ARTICHOKE CASSEROLE

3 tbsp. butter or oleo	1 lb. canned or frozen
1½ cups milk	artichoke hearts
⅛ tsp. pepper	Buttered bread crumbs
3 6 oz. cans crabmeat or	3 tbsp. flour
1 pound frozen King crab	1 tsp. salt
	2 tbsp. sherry

Make cream sauce of butter, flour and milk. Add seasonings, sherry, crabmeat and cooked artichoke hearts. Pour into greased casserole. Top with crumbs. Bake at 350° for 30-40 minutes.

Recipe may be doubled. Serves 6.

Erla Pauole

CHEESE CASSEROLE

A light luncheon or supper dish with a green salad, fruit or a green vegetable.

7 slices of bread, buttered lightly.

1. Cut 2 of the slices twice across the bias, making 8 triangular pieces. Cut the remaining bread into cubes – there should be about 4 cups.
2. Place the cubed bread in a buttered casserole. Sprinkle with 1 cup shredded, aged Cheddar cheese.
3. Combine and beat:

2 eggs	1 cup milk
1 tsp. salt	¼ tsp. paprika
few shakes of cayenne	½ tsp. dry mustard

If desired: 1 tsp. grated onion and 1 tbsp. minced parsley or chives.
4. Pour these ingredients over the cheese. Place the triangles of bread around the casserole edge to form a crown.
5. Bake at 350° for 25 minutes. Serve at once.

Serves 4.

Beverly Hansen

WILD RICE CASSEROLE

1 pkg. long grain wild rice	½ cup brown rice
¾ lb. sharp cheddar cheese	2 diced onions
1 lge. green pepper, diced	1 cube butter
1 10 oz. can chopped mushrooms	1 cup half and half

Cook rice according to package directions, with ½ cup brown rice. Add 1 tsp. salt.

Saute onions, pepper and mushrooms in 1 cube butter. Mix all together reserving enough cheese for top of casserole. Top with cheese and pour half-and-half over. Bake at 400° for 30 minutes. Very good with turkey dinner. Serves 8-10.

Alice M Johnson

QUICHE LORAINE

2 cups flour	1-2 cups milk
½ cup margarine	½ cup Swiss cheese
½ tsp. sugar	1 cup American cheese
3-4 tbsp. water	½ cup Monterey cheese
½ lb. bacon	1 cup chopped onions
6-8 eggs	1 tsp. cream of wheat

Make dough with flour, margarine, sugar and water. Form a ball then roll it out to fit a pan 9x13 in. Pour cream of wheat on and let stand. Fry bacon. Fry onions in drippings. Spread onions over cream of wheat. Top with bacon, mixed grated cheeses. Bake in 350°-375° oven for 15 minutes.

Beat eggs and milk and pour over the cheese. Bake for 30-35 minutes more or till brown.

Suggestion: Do not preheat oven for more than 5 minutes.

For Vegetable Quiche: substitute mushroom, spinach, or zucchini for bacon.

Sophie Perrenoud

EGGPLANT CASSEROLE

2½ cups diced eggplant (after peeling)

1. In a skillet pour ⅓ cup olive oil. Saute until softened – ¾ cup finely sliced onions and 2 cloves minced garlic.

2. Add: ½ cup whole pitted black olives.
   4 julienned green peppers with seeds and membranes removed.
   3 cups zucchini in ½ inch slices.
   2 cups skinned, seeded, quartered tomatoes.

3. Add the eggplant.

4. Add ½ tsp. oregano or 2 tsp. chopped fresh basil.

5. Simmer, uncovered, over very low heat for about 30 minutes to reduce the liquid. Cover and heat about 20 minutes longer.

6. Add salt and grated fresh pepper.

Serves 8.

Beverly Hansen

SAVORY CRESCENT ROLL

3 oz. Philadelphia
  cream cheese
2 tbsp. oleo
1 tbsp. chopped onion
1 can crescent rolls

2 cups chicken, cooked and
  cut into small pieces
Add salt and pepper to taste
2 tbsp. milk
1 tbsp. pimiento
¾ cups croutons

Heat oven to 350°. Mix cheese and oleo until creamy. Add together the chicken, milk, onions and pimiento and mix well. Divide crescent rolls into 4 pieces and put equal amount of mixture into center of each. Draw up corners and twist together. Roll in crushed croutons and brush with melted butter lightly. Place on cooky sheet and bake until lightly browned. Yummy! Serves 4.

Bobbi Gardner

ZUCCHINI SAUSAGE TORTE

2 lbs. zucchini
  (you can use frozen)
½ lb. pork sausage
½ cup cracker crumbs
½ cup grated Parmesan cheese

pinch of thyme and rosemary
garlic salt, salt and
  pepper to taste
½ cup chopped onion
2 eggs, beaten

Boil zucchini until tender. Drain well and chop. Cook sausage and onion together until sausage browns. Stir and break sausage into bits.

Add zucchini, all other ingredients and ½ of the cheese. Mix well.

Turn into greased 9 in. pie plate. Sprinkle with remaining cheese. Bake at 350° until firm – about 45 minutes. Serves 4-6.

Beverly Schulte

CASSEROLE LASAGNE

1 lb. lean ground beef
⅓ cup chopped onion
⅓ cup chopped celery
2 6 oz. cans tomato paste
1 6 oz. can tomato sauce
1 tsp. oregano
1 tsp. basil
1 tsp. Worcestershire

1 cup cottage cheese
1 cup sour cream
3 cups broad noodles,
   cooked and drained
¼ lb. sliced Mozzarella cheese
¼ tsp. Tabasco
Salt and pepper to taste

1. In a large skillet brown the beef in a little oil.
2. Reduce heat and add onion, celery and green pepper. Saute gently for a few minutes.
3. Blend in tomato paste and sauce with the seasonings. Cook gently and stir well for about 10 min.
4. Mix sour cream with the cooked noodles. Layer half into buttered casserole.
5. Add half of the tomato mixture. Place slices of Mozzarella cheese over the meat. Spoon on half of the cottage cheese.
6. Repeat the layers.
7. Bake at 350° for 35 to 40 minutes. Serves 6.

Beverly Hansen

MINI PIZZA

1 lb. ground beef
1 16 oz. can tomato paste
3½ tbsp. A1 steak sauce
1 tsp. Italian herb seasoning
6-8 English muffins,
   split and toasted

1¾ cups mozzarella cheese
Grated Parmesan cheese
¼ cup sliced green onion
⅜ cups minced onion

In a medium skillet cook and crumble meat. Drain. Add onion and cook until soft. Mix in tomato paste, steak sauce, and Italian herb seasoning. Spread muffins with meat. Top with cheese and green onion. Put on baking sheet. Broil 2 to 4 minutes or until cheese is melted. 6-8 servings.

Barbara Theus

LANI'S ORIENTAL SURPRISE

1 medium eggplant, or
   1 pkg. sliced eggplant
8 oz. fresh mushrooms
1-2 lbs. green beans
2-3 lbs. beef or pork
1 packet Japanese meat
   soup base

1 packet Japanese vegetable
   soup base
1 large green pepper
3 carrots
2 sticks butter
1 round onion

Wash all vegetables before slicing slantwise. Put all vegetables in strainer. Wash and cut onion in half, then slice. Put onion in separate container, covered with water. Melt butter in a skillet. When butter is melted, add vegetables. Sprinkle 1 packet vegetable soup base over vegetables. Add onion and cook together until tender. Do not overcook.

In another skillet melt butter and add sliced beef or pork. Sprinkle meat soup base over meat. Cook until golden brown – about 1 minute. Remove meat from pan. Stir in same pan 1 tbsp. flour, ½ cup water and a dash of shoyu. Cook until thickened. Mix gravy, meat and vegetables. Let stand for 5 min. Serve with rice.

Lani Jury

HOMINY CASSEROLE

1 #2½ can white hominy
1 stick butter, or margarine
3 tbsp. vermouth

Salt and pepper to taste
1 pt. sour cream
Grated cheddar cheese

Saute hominy in butter with salt and pepper. Add all ingredients except cheese. Heat through. Place in casserole and top with cheese. Bake at 350° until cheese is bubbly.

Margaret Montgomery

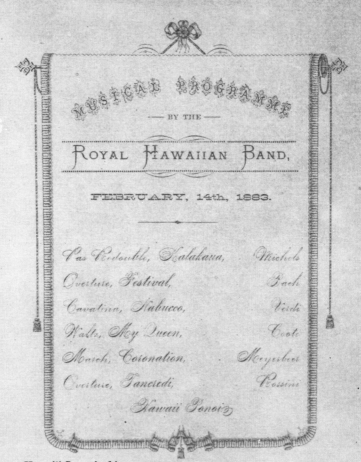

MUSICAL PROGRAMME

— BY THE —

ROYAL HAWAIIAN BAND,

FEBRUARY, 14th, 1883.

Pas Redouble, Kalakaua,	Michols
Overture, Festival,	Bach
Cavatina, Nabucco,	Verdi
Waltz, My Queen,	Coote
March, Coronation,	Meyerbeer
Overture, Tancredi,	Rossini
Hawaii Ponoi,	

NOTES

MEA ONO PANIOLO − Cowboy coffeecake

2⅓ cups sifted enriched flour   ½ tsp. salt
2 cups raw brown sugar   ⅔ cup shortening
2 tsp. baking powder   ½ tsp. soda
½ tsp. cinnamon   ½ tsp. nutmeg
1 cup buttermilk   ½ cup macadamia nuts
2 well-beaten eggs

Combine flour, salt, sugar and shortening. Mix until crumbly. Reserve ½ cup of the mixture.

To remaining crumbs, add baking powder, soda and spices. Mix thoroughly. Add milk and eggs. Mix well. Pour into 2 wax paper-lined 8x8x2 in. baking pans. Sprinkle with reserved crumbs. Sprinkle chopped nuts and cinnamon on top. Bake at 375° for 25-30 min.

Florence Kelley

APPLE SHORTBREAD

Crust: 1½ cups butter   1 cup sugar
     4 cups flour

Filling: 3 cups diced apples   ¼ cup flour
     ½ cup sugar   1 tbsp. fresh lemon juice
     1½ tsp. cinnamon

Cream together butter and sugar. Add flour all at once. Mix well. Press half of dough into a 9x13 inch greased pan.

Combine filling ingredients and pour over crust.

Sprinkle remainder of dough over apple filling.

Bake at 375° for 45 minutes.

Raynelle Theus

PARTY MUFFINS

Large box of raisin bran   3 cups sugar
5 cups flour   5 tsp. baking soda
2 tsp. salt

Mix all dry ingredients. In large bowl add:
1 cup oil   1 qt. buttermilk
4 eggs, well beaten

Mix all together. For party treats add nuts and extra raisin. Also glazed fruit for color. Bake in small muffin pans ¾ full about 20 min. at 400°. Makes about 15 dozen. May keep in refrigerator.

Henry Piltz Kramer

WHOLE WHEAT QUICK BREAD

A lady who served as hairdresser and assistant to the cook in the royal household of Queen Victoria brought this recipe with her to the USA. My great-grandmother and grandmother gave the recipe to me.

1 egg, beaten   2 cups buttermilk
3 tbsp. molasses or honey   1½ tbsp. melted butter
2 cups whole wheat flour   1 tsp. soda
1 tsp. salt   1 tsp. baking powder
½ cup nuts   ½ cup raisins

Combine eggs, buttermilk, molasses and melted butter. Stir in dry ingredients that have been mixed together. Stir in nuts and raisins. Spoon batter into 2 greased loaf pans. Bake at 400° for 1 hour. Cool.

Diane Clark

STRAWBERRIES AND CREAM BREAD

1¾ cups all purpose flour
½ tsp. baking powder
½ tsp. salt
½ cup butter
½ cup sour cream – at room
   temp. – with butter, eggs

¾ cup sugar
1 cup strawberries,
   coarsely chopped
¼ tsp. baking soda
¼ tsp. cinnamon
2 eggs
1 tsp. vanilla

Grease 8x4 in. loaf pan. Preheat oven to 350°. In large bowl combine dry ingredients, except sugar.

In small bowl cream butter with electric mixer. Gradually add sugar. Beat till airy (about 1 min.) Add eggs one at a time. Then beat in sour cream and vanilla. Stir into dry ingredients only until moistened. Add strawberries. Turn into pan, smooth top and bake 60-65 min. Leave in pan for 10 min. then turn out onto a rack to cool.

Wendy Burkholder

HUSH PUPPIES FOR FOUR

2½ cups corn meal
1 tbsp. salt
2 eggs
1 sm. onion, chopped or diced

1 cup flour
1 tbsp. baking soda
1 can 7 Up

Mix to pancake texture. Heat cooking oil to 375°. Use large spoon to put batter into hot cooking oil. Cook until golden brown.

Milton Ross

CORN BREAD – QUICK AND EASY

3 cups Bisquick
½ cup corn meal
1 tsp. baking powder
1 cup sugar

1½ cups milk
¾ cup oil
1 tsp. vanilla
3 eggs

Mix dry ingredients. Add all wet ingredients together. Mix. Cook at 350° in 12x9x2 in. pan for 35-45 min. Melt ¼ lb. of butter on top while warm.

Henry Piltz Kramer

POPPY SEED BREAD

Beat 4 eggs.
Add: 1½ cups oil   1 cup chopped nuts (optional)
    1½ tsp. baking soda   3 cups flour
    2 cups sugar   ½ tsp. salt
    1 12 oz. can evaporated   1 2 oz. box poppy seeds
      milk

Mix all ingredients together and pour into a greased 10 inch tube pan or 2 loaf pans.

Bake at 350° for 1 hour and 15 minutes. Let cool 20-30 minutes before removing from pan.

Dawn Krause

SCONES

1 egg   ⅓ cup buttermilk or milk
Pinch "Equal"   2 cups bisquick
Add chopped dates or raisins

Don't knead. Just toss. Cut with a biscuit cutter.

Bake 10 minutes at 450°.

Doug Gibson

PRIZE BISCUITS

Sift together:

2 cups flour   4 tsp. baking powder
2 tsp. sugar   ½ tsp. salt
½ tsp. cream of tartar

Cut in: ½ cup shortening and add ⅔ cup milk all at once. Stir until dough follows fork around bowl. (Dough should be soft, easy to handle).

Turn dough onto lightly floured surface. Knead gently 8 or 10 times. Bake at 450°. Makes 2 doz.

Mary Kirkham

MANGO BREAD

2 cups flour
½ cup shredded canned
    coconut
2 cups chopped ripe mangos**
2 eggs, beaten
1½ cups sugar

½ cup chopped macadamia nuts
¾ cup oil
1 tsp. cinnamon
2 tsp. soda
2 tsp. vanilla

Preheat oven to 350°. Grease and flour 9x3 in. loaf pan.

Sift flour with soda and cinnamon into mixing bowl. Stir in sugar, coconut and nuts. Add remaining ingredients and mix well. Pour into pan and bake 1¼ hours.

**For Banana Bread substitute 1½ cups mashed ripe bananas.

Sally McClellan

AUG. 6, 1890

Dinner at Iolani Palace

IN HONOR OF

Rear Admiral George Brown.

AUGUST 6TH, 1890.

NOTES

DATE-APRICOT BAR COOKIES

Filling: 1 cup cut-up dates   ½ cup sugar
     2 cups mashed, cooked dried apricots, drained. A package
     of 12 oz. of dried apricots is right.
     ¼ cup of apricot cooking water.

1. Mix all ingredients in a saucepan.
2. Cook over low heat, stirring constantly until thickened (about 5 minutes)
3. Cool. Set aside.

Cookies: ¾ cup soft shortening
     1 cup brown sugar   1¾ cups sifted flour
     ½ tsp. soda   ½ tsp. salt
     1½ cups rolled oats

1. Cream shortening. Add sugar and cream in well.
2. Sift and measure flour. Sift 2 or 3 times with soda and salt.
3. Add flour mixture and oats. Mix together well.
4. Place half of the crumb mixture in a greased and floured 8x11 inch oblong cake pan. Press and flatten with hands to cover the pan bottom.
5. Spread cooled filling over the crumb bottom.
6. Sprinkle remaining crumbs over the surface, patting gently.
7. Bake until lightly browned – about 30-35 minutes at 350°.
8. Cut into bars while still warm. Makes 2½ dozen 1½ x 2 inch bars.

Beverly Hansen

RYE HAPPIES

½ cup unsifted rye flour   1 tsp. vanilla
½ tsp. salt   ½ cup Quick Oats
⅓ cup oil   ½ tsp. baking powder
¾-1 cup coarsely ground   1 cup packed brown sugar
  almonds   2 eggs

Preheat oven to 350°. Grease well 9 in. square pan. Beat eggs, oil and vanilla. Add brown sugar and beat until free of lumps. Stir in dry ingredients and mix well. Bake 30-35 min. Cool, cut in squares. Dust with powdered sugar, optional.

Alice Johnson

BROWN SUGAR CHEWS (HAOLE BROWNIES)

1 egg
1 cup brown sugar
1 tsp. vanilla
½ cup sifted flour

¼ tsp. salt
¼ tsp. baking soda
1 cup chopped walnuts

Blend egg, sugar and vanilla. Add the sifted flour, salt and soda. Add walnuts. Bake 18 to 20 min. in a greased 9x9 inch pan at 350°. After baking, cool and cut into squares.

Don Hebert

OATMEAL CRISPIES

1 cup butter or margarine, softened
1 cup sugar
2 eggs, beaten
2 cups all purpose flour
1 tsp. salt
2 cups uncooked regular oats

1 6 oz. pkge. peanut butter chips
1 6 oz. pkge. butterscotch chips
1 cup packed brown sugar
1 cup peanut butter
1 tsp. soda
1 tsp. vanilla

Cream butter, peanut butter and sugar until light and fluffy. Add eggs, blending well. Combine flour, soda and salt. Add to creamed mixture, mixing well. Stir in vanilla, chips and oats. Drop dough by half teaspoonfuls on greased cooky sheets. Bake at 350° about 8-10 min. or until lightly browned. Remove to wire racks immediately. Makes 5 dozen.

Nancy Hicks

CHOCOLATE CANDY LACY CRISPS

Boil ½ cup light corn syrup.
Add ⅓ cup butter and 4 oz. Bakers German chocolate.
Stir over low heat until smooth.
Remove from heat and stir in:
    ½ cup light brown sugar, firmly packed
    1 cup flour
    ⅔ cup coconut

Drop from a tablespoon onto lightly greased baking sheets, 3 inches apart. Bake at 300° for 15 minutes or until wafers bubble vigorously and have lacy holes. Cool for 2 minutes. Finish cooling on racks, or roll wafers over a wooden spoon handle, cool, fill with sweetened whipped cream.

Makes 2½ dozen.

Ruth Bradford

OATMEAL SCOTCHIES PAN COOKIES

1 cup all purpose flour
½ tsp. salt
1 cup butter, softened
⅝ cup packed brown sugar
¾ tsp. vanilla
3 cups oats, uncooked, either quick or old fashion
1 12 oz. pkg. butterscotch bits

1 tsp. baking soda
½ tsp. cinnamon
⅝ cup sugar
2 eggs

In small bowl, combine flour, baking soda, salt and cinnamon. Set aside. In large bowl combine butter, sugar, brown sugar, eggs and vanilla. Beat until light and airy. Gradually add flour mixture. Stir in oats and butterscotch bits. Add ½ cup nuts if desired. Spread into greased 15x10x1 inch baking pan. Bake at 375° for 20-25 minutes. Cool. Cut into squares. Makes 3 dozen 2 inch squares.

Barbara Theus

UNDAGI – Okinawan Doughnut

3 cups flour
1 cup sugar
3 eggs
½ tsp. salt

1½ tsp. baking powder
1 tbsp. butter
1 cup milk
1 tsp. vanilla

Sift flour and all dry ingredients well. Mix eggs, milk and vanilla together. Pour into dry ingredients while mixing. Mix in butter. Drop balls of batter into hot oil and deep fry. Makes 2-3 dozen.

Colleen Murakami

BOURBON BALLS

2 lbs. confectioner's sugar
1 stick butter
½ cup bourbon
12 oz. pkg. of chocolate chips
   or 8 oz. unsweetened bits
   and 4 squares bitter chocolate

¼ bar paraffin
1 cup chopped pecans

Blend the confectioner's sugar with melted butter. Soak the pecans in the bourbon. Mix together with hands. Form into bite size balls and place on a cooky sheet in the refrigerator to chill. Melt the chocolate and paraffin (double boiler works best as it keeps the temperature constant). Dip balls into chocolate mixture and chill. A fork works fine.

Jane Horn

PEANUT BUTTER BALLS

2 boxes powdered sugar
2 sticks margarine, softened
12 oz. chocolate chips

Dash of vanilla
3 cups peanut butter
¼ bar paraffin

Mix peanut butter and margarine, adding sugar slowly until mixture is stiff. (I use a mixer.) Roll into 1 inch balls. Dip into 12 oz. melted chocolate into which has been added ¼ bar of paraffin. Keep chocolate mixture warm over double boiler. Tastes like peanut butter cups.

Jane Horn

MOLASSES REFRIGERATOR COOKIES

1943 – from Miss Annie and Miss Bertha of the 'Plumeria Tea Room' on Wilder Ave. Miss Annie and Miss Bertha originally cooked and baked for the Salvation Army's 'Waioli Tea Room.'

1½ cups shortening (like Crisco)
1½ tsp. vanilla
1½ cups brown sugar, firmly packed
¾ cup dark molasses
1 large egg

Cream and mix well. Add: 6 cups flour sifted with
½ tsp. salt   3 tsp. baking powder

Pack into 3 rolls, chill, slice thin. Bake at 350° for 9 to 12 minutes.

Anne Jurczynski

MOLASSES CRINKLE COOKIES

¾ cup soft shortening   2¼ cups sifted flour
1 cup brown sugar   2 tsp. soda
1 egg   ¼ tsp. salt
¼ cup molasses   ½ tsp. cloves
1 tsp. cinnamon   1 tsp. ginger

1. Cream shortening well.
2. Add the sugar and cream together.
3. Add a beaten egg with the molasses. Mix.
4. Sift flour. Measure. Sift 2 or 3 times with all other dry ingredients.
5. Add flour mixture to shortening mixture, stir.
6. Chill dough.
7. Roll into balls the size of large walnuts. Dip 1 side in sugar; place, sugared side up, 3 inches apart on greased cookie sheet.
8. Sprinkle a few drops of water on each surface. (It helps produce a crinkled surface.)
9. Bake until just set but not hard – 10 to 12 minutes at 375°. Makes 4 dozen 2½ inch cookies.

Beverly Hansen

NORWEGIAN WHITE PEPPERNUTS

1 cup butter
4 egg yolks
2 cups flour
1 tsp. nutmeg
¼ tsp. white pepper

1 cup sugar
1 cup chopped almonds
1 tsp. cinnamon
¼ tsp. cloves

Cream butter, sugar, egg yolks. Add spices to sifted flour and combine with creamed mixture.

Form dough into small balls. Bake in 375° oven until brown. When removed from baking sheet, roll in powdered sugar.

Helen V. Rantala

SESAME SEED COOKIES

¾ cup sesame seeds – toast for 5 minutes.
Add: ½ cup coconut – toast 5 minutes more. (Do not over-brown).

Sift 2 cups flour with 1 tsp. baking powder, ½ tsp. soda, ½ tsp. salt.

Cream ¾ cup butter, 1 cup brown sugar, 1 egg, 1 tsp. vanilla. Add sesame seeds and coconut. Mix well. Add dry ingredients and mix well. Chill dough. Shape into balls, put on ungreased cooky sheet. Press down with floured bottom of glass. Bake for 10 minutes at 350°.

Helen V. Rantala

FINNISH LEMON BUTTER COOKIES

Beat together for 3-4 minutes:
2 eggs, ⅔ cup sugar, ½ tsp. vanilla. *Add:* 2 tsp. grated lemon rind (½ tsp., more if you like tart cookies).

Beat: ¾ stick unsalted butter until light and fluffy. *Add* to sugar/egg mixture, alternately with ⅔ cup flour.

Drop by tsp. on buttered cooky sheet 2-3 in. apart. Flatten into 2 in. rounds with spoon dipped in water. Bake at 400° for 5 mins. until edges are light brown.

Helen V. Rantala

ENERGY BARS

Butter a 10½x10½x⅝ inch pan.

Step 1: In a large bowl measure
2 cups unsalted roasted peanuts
1 cup raisins
½ cup chopped dried apricots (optional)

Step 2: Toast or heat in order
1 cup raw sunflower seeds
1 cup raw sesame seeds
2½ cups quick oats
3½ cups crisp rice cereal

Step 3: Melt in pan, stirring constantly
½ stick margarine or butter
½ cup peanut butter
1 10 oz. pkg. miniature marshmallows

Combine Step 1 with Step 2 mixtures. Mix well and pour melted Step 3 caramel mixture into Step 1 and 2 mixtures. Mix well. *Work fast.* Pour into buttered pan, using hands or rolling pin to flatten. Cut into bars or squares. Yield: About 50.

Nancy Hicks

JO'S LEMON BARS

1 cup butter or margarine   ½ cup powdered sugar
2 cups flour

Mix. Line a 9x14 inch greased pan. Bake at 350° for 15 minutes.

Blend: 4 eggs, slightly beaten
       2 cups white sugar
       4 tbsp. lemon juice
       2 tsp. lemon rind
       4 tbsp. flour
       1 tsp. baking powder
       2 drops lemon extract

Pour over the crust in pan. Bake at 350° for 22 minutes. Let cool a few minutes. Sprinkle powdered sugar over all. Loosen around edges. Cut in squares.

Luana McKenney

"BETTER THAN BOUGHT COOKIES"

2 cups brown sugar	5 cups quick oats
2 cups white sugar	1 tsp. salt
1 lb. butter	2 tsp. soda
4 eggs	2 tsp. vanilla
4 cups flour	3 cups chopped nuts

2 12 oz. pkgs. chocolate or butterscotch chips

Cream first 4 ingredients together. Add the rest. Mix well. Roll batter into golf ball sized portions. Pat down into ungreased pan. Bake at 400° for 6-7 minutes. Do not overcook!

Beverly Schulte

MANDEL KRANSAR (SWEDISH COOKIES)

1½ cups powdered sugar	1 lb. butter
2 eggs	4 cups flour

¼ lb. bitter almonds grated and ½ lb. sweet almonds, grated

Mix well and squeeze through a pastry bag in circles. Put on ungreased cookie sheet. Bake in medium oven for about 12 minutes.

Olive Linde

WONDER BAR

Mix together: 2 cups crushed graham crackers
                1 cup coconut
                1 cup walnut pieces

Mix together: in a saucepan: ½ cup butter
                       ½ cup sugar
                       1 beaten egg

Heat and stir the butter, sugar, egg mixture until bubbly. Mix it with the crumb mixture and spread into 8x12 baking pan.

Make a frosting of ¼ cup butter, 1 cup powdered sugar, 1 tsp. vanilla and 1 tbsp. milk. Spread this over the first layer.

Allow the mixture to set long enough for the frosting to harden a little. Then, melt 6 standard Hershey Bars and spread over the top. You now have 3 layers. Cut into small squares and serve.

Mary Kirkham

MOLASSES SUGAR COOKIES

¾ cup shortening
1 cup sugar
¼ cup molasses
1 egg
2 cups sifted flour

2 tsp. baking soda
1 tsp. cinnamon
½ tsp. cloves
½ tsp. ginger
½ tsp. salt

Cream together shortening and sugar. Add molasses and egg. Beat well. Sift together flour, soda, cinnamon, cloves, ginger and salt. Add to first mixture. Mix well. Chill. Form in 1 inch balls, roll in granulated sugar and place on greased cooky sheets 2 inch apart. Bake at 375° for 8-10 minutes.

Nancy Hicks

BUTTER NUT CHEWIES

½ tsp. salt
2 eggs
1 tsp. vanilla
1½ cups unsifted all purpose
flour

1 cup finely chopped nuts
⅓ cup butter, melted
2 cups packed brown sugar
2 tsp. baking powder

Preheat oven to 350°. Grease 13x9x2 inch pan with butter-flavored Crisco.

Beat eggs until light and airy in large bowl of electric mixer. Beat in sugar, vanilla and butter until creamy. Combine flour with baking powder and salt. Add to egg mixture. Mix at low speed until blended. Stir in nuts at low speed. Mixture will be stiff.

Spread evenly in prepared pan. Bake at 350° for 25-30 minutes or until top is light brown. Cool 10-15 minutes. Cut into bars. Makes 24.

Barbara Theus

Menu.

HORS D'ŒUVRE.

Saucisse de Boulogne.   Caviar Pate.

Anchovies.

SOUPIERRES.

Sherry Amontilado.   Green Turtle.   Consomme ala Reine.

POISSONS.

Chateau D'Iquem.
1878.   Boiled Uhu   Fried Amaama

ENTREES.

Johanisberg Castle.
Prince Metternich.   Salmi of Ducks aux Olives.   Pigeons au Cresson.
Chateau.
1876 Vintage.

RÔTS.

"Chateau Lafite."   Turkey.   Ham, Champagne Sauce.
1877 Vintage.
Fillet of Beef aux Champignons.

PUNCH ALA ROMAINE.

CURRIES.

Chambertin.
Romano.   Shrimp.   Chicken.
1874 Vintage

SALAD ALA RUSSE.

ENTREMENTS.

Champagne   Pudding ala Diplomate.   Sambio Glace.
Ruinart Pere et Fils.
Magnums 1874 Vintage.   Strawberry and Vanilla Ice Cream.

Fruits.

Curacoa (Special)
Benedictine.   CAFE.
Grand Champagne.
Cognac 1825 Vintage.

NOTES

CAKES

SWEDISH CARDAMOM CAKE

1 cube margarine
2 cups sugar
1 cup milk or cream
2 tsp. ground cinnamon

2 eggs
2 cups flour
2 tsp. ground cardamom
2 tsp. baking powder

Cream sugar and margarine. Add eggs and beat well until smooth and creamy. Mix flour with baking powder, cardamom and cinnamon and add to batter alternating with the milk. Bake in tube pan for about 45 minutes at 350°. Serves about 8.

Elsa Nilsson

PUMPKIN CRUNCH CAKE

1 large can solid pumpkin
1 13 oz. can evaporated milk
1 cup sugar
1 tsp. cinnamon
3 eggs, beaten
1 box yellow cake mix
2 quarter pound sticks of butter
1 cup chopped macadamia nuts

Line a 9x13 in. cake pan with wax paper. Mix together pumpkin, milk, sugar, cinnamon and eggs. Pour into pan. Sprinkle cake mix over mixture and spread nuts on top.

Melt butter, cool slightly and pour over all. Bake 1 hour at 350° or until top is golden brown. Cool 5-10 minutes. Turn over cake on serving dish. Remove wax paper. Top with whipped cream or Cool Whip, if desired.

Margaret Montgomery

PUA'S CAKE OR A CAKE TO CARRY

Cake: Prepare a Duncan Hines Supreme Orange cake or yellow cake mix as directed but add the rind of 1 orange, finely grated. Bake in a larger than 9x13 inch pan – a roasting pan is fine. Cook about 20 minutes. Cool in pan.

Filling: Mix 1 8 oz. pkg. cream cheese with 1½ cups milk and 1 pkg. instant coconut pudding. Don't worry about any small lumps. Spread on cake IMMEDIATELY. Top with 2 cans well drained mandarin oranges or combination of mango slices and bananas. Even fresh oranges in thin sections will be good. Try crushed pineapple.

Top: Spread 1½ containers of Cool Whip or 2 pkgs. of Dream Whip. Sprinkle with a small package of coconut which has been moistened with 2 tbsp. milk.

Chill whole cake. Travels well and serves over 20.

Claire Hiett Gregorcyk

AUNT ESTHER'S ORANGE CAKE

1½ cups sugar
¾ cup butter
2 eggs
2 cups flour
1 level tsp. baking soda
1 tsp. nutmeg

¾ cups sour milk
1 cup raisins, chopped
2 medium oranges
½ cup chopped nuts
1 tsp. cinnamon

Cream sugar and butter, add eggs and soda and milk, then the flour, cinnamon and nutmeg.

Grind the pulp and rind of oranges after squeezing out the juice. Mix pulp and rind with nuts and raisins, add to the batter. Put into loaf pan in 350° oven for 45 minutes to 1 hour.

After removing cake from the pan pour the orange juice over and let it soak in. Frost with butter cream frosting made with orange juice. Sprinkle grated rind on top.

Olive Linde

CALIFORNIA PUMPKIN CAKE

1 lge. can pumpkin	½ tsp cloves
1½ cups sugar	1 lge. can evaporated milk
½ tsp. salt	4 eggs
1 tsp. fresh grated ginger	2 tsp. cinnamon

Mix all together. Place in ungreased 9x14 inch Pyrex dish.

1 box yellow cake mix sprinkled on top of mixture
1 cup chopped nuts
2 sticks melted butter over all

Bake at 350° for 1 hour. Serves 6.

Jeanne Read Alden

VI'S HAWAIIAN CREAM CAKE

2 cups sugar	1 cup buttermilk
1 stick margarine	1 tsp. soda
½ cup Crisco oil	1 cup coconut
5 egg yolks	5 egg whites
2 cups flour	1 cup pecans or walnuts
1 tsp. vanilla	

Prepare 3 cake pans – grease, flour and line with wax paper.

Blend sugar with Crisco oil and margarine. Add egg yolks. Mix. Combine flour with mixture. Stir in buttermilk, soda, coconut and vanilla.

Beat egg whites until stiff, then fold into mixture. Add nuts. Bake at 325° for 25 minutes or until cake tests done.

Icing:
1 8 oz. pkg. cream cheese (room temperature)

1 stick margarine	1 tsp. vanilla
1 box confectioners sugar	1 cup chopped nuts

Blend cream cheese, margarine and sugar until smooth. Add vanilla and nuts. Spread on cake.

Vi-Lani Robertson

STONEHENGE CHOCOLATE

½ cup seedless raisins
1 cup sugar
10 1 oz. squares unsweetened chocolate, cut up
¾ cup butter

1 cup ground blanched almonds
½ cup flour
⅔ cup bourbon whiskey
¼ cup water
6 eggs, separated

Soak raisins in whiskey. Boil sugar and water together. Remove from heat and stir in chocolate until chocolate melts. Cool. With electric mixer beat butter until softened. Beat in egg yolks, one at a time. With mixer on low speed, add half the chocolate mixture, then half the ground almonds. Repeat. Add whiskey and raisins. Beat in flour.

Beat egg whites until stiff. Fold egg whites into batter.

Line bottom of a 9 inch tube spring-form pan with wax paper. Grease and flour. Bake at 375° for 30 minutes. Frost if desired.

Vi-Lani Robertson

CARROT CAKE

2 cups flour
2 cups sugar
2 tsp. cinnamon
2 tsp. baking soda
1 tsp. salt

3 cups finely grated carrots
4 eggs
1½ cups fresh Wesson oil
2 tsp. baking powder
½ cup nuts

Sift flour, sugar, cinnamon, salt, soda and baking powder.

Add eggs and oil. Beat until smooth. Add carrots and nuts. Mix well.

Bake at 350° for 35-40 minutes in 3 8 inch pans, greased and floured.

Icing:
½ stick margarine or butter
8 oz. pkg. cream cheese
¾ box powdered (10X) sugar
2 tsp. vanilla

Nancy Hicks

SCRIPTURE CAKE

1 cup Judges 5:25	Butter
2 cups Jeremiah 6:20	Sugar
3½ cups First Kings 4:22	Flour
2 cups First Samuel 30:12	Raisins
2 cups First Samuel 30:12	Figs
1 cup Genesis 43:11	Almonds
1 cup Genesis 24:20	Water
6 Isaiah 10:14	Eggs
1 tbsp. Exodus 16:31	Honey
Pinch of Leviticus 2:13	Salt
To taste: 1 Kings 10:2	Spices

Follow Solomon's advice in Proverbs 23:14:

Chop raisins, figs, and almonds. Sift flour, salt and sugar together. Cream in butter. Beat in water and eggs. Add figs, raisins and almonds. Stir in honey and spices. Mix well. Pour into greased tube pan. Bake at 350° for 50-60 minutes.

Diane Clark

LEMON DELIGHT

Bottom layer - Crust
1½ cups flour   1½ sticks butter
¾ cup walnuts, chopped

Mix and spread into 13x9 inch pan. Bake 15-20 minutes in 350° oven. Cool.

Second layer
8 oz. cream cheese   1 cup powdered sugar
1 cup Cool Whip, from 8 oz. container

Mix softened cream cheese with sugar. Mix in Cool Whip. Spread over crust. Chill.

Third layer
3 boxes instant lemon pudding. 4 cups milk

Mix together until thickened. Spread over cream cheese layer. Chill.

Top layer
Spread remainder of Cool Whip over pudding. Top with chopped walnuts.

Freida Theus

OATMEAL CAKE

1 cup quick oats   1⅓ cup boiling water
Pour water over oats and let stand while continuing

Cream together: 1 cup brown sugar (preferably dark)
1 cup white sugar   ½ cup shortening (not butter)

Add 2 eggs and beat. *Sift together:*
1⅓ cups flour   1 tsp. soda
1 tsp. cinnamon   pinch of salt

Mix with the above. Stir in the oatmeal.

Pour into a 9x13 inch cake pan. Preheat oven to 350°. Bake for 30-40 minutes.

Topping:
Mix together: 6 tbsp. melted butter
½ cup brown sugar   ½ cup pecans or walnuts
¼ cup evaporated milk   (may use more)
1 cup coconut   ½ tsp. nutmeg
½ tsp. vanilla

While cake is still hot, spread topping over it and broil until it is bubbly and slightly brown. WATCH CAREFULLY as it burns easily.

Betty Bowyer

TROPICAL GINGERBREAD

½ cup shortening   1 tsp. cinnamon
½ cup sugar   1 tsp. ginger
1 egg   ½ tsp. cloves
2½ cups flour   ½ tsp. salt
1½ tsp. baking soda   1 cup molasses
1 cup hot water

Cream together shortening and sugar. Add egg and beat well. Sift together flour, baking soda, spices and salt. Combine molasses and water. Add alternately with flour to first mixture. Pour into a greased wax paper lined 9x9x2 inch pan. Bake at 350° 35-40 minutes. Cool 5 minutes. Remove from pan. Cover with white frosting and sprinkle generously with coconut. Can also be served with whipped cream.

Nancy Hicks

MY MOTHER'S RECIPE FOR PAPRIKA CAKE

2 eggs   ½ cup butter
1½ cup sugar   1 cup sour milk
⅔ tsp. baking soda   2 cups cake flour

Separate eggs, cream butter and sugar. Add egg yolks. Add milk and baking soda. Alternate with flour. Add beaten egg whites. Bake at 350° until toothpick stuck in center comes out clean. Cool cake layers. (Grease and flour pans before baking.)

Frosting:
2 tbsp. melted butter
1 cup whipping cream with powdered sugar to thicken
1 tsp. paprika
Shredded coconut

Combine cool whipping cream, which has been sweetened with powdered sugar to thicken. Add paprika. Frost cake. Sprinkle with shredded coconut.

                                                    Mako Vance

BANANA PIE

4 cups sliced bananas, ripe but firm
½ cup pineapple juice   ½ cup sugar
1 tsp. cinnamon   1 tbsp. butter or margarine

Soak sliced bananas in pineapple juice for 20 to 30 minutes. Drain, saving the pineapple juice. Place bananas in pastry lined pie plate. Add sugar and cinnamon which have been mixed together. Add 2 tbsp. of the pineapple juice drained from bananas. Dot with butter and cover with top crust. Bake at 400° for 30-45 min. or until crust browns. 1 9 inch pie.

Julia Toomey

BANANA CREAM PIE

Crust:
1 cup flour   1 stick Imperial margarine
2 tbsp. sugar   ½ cup chopped nuts

Press into 9x13 inch or 9 inch round pan. Prick with fork. Bake at 325° until slightly brown. Cool.

Line pastry with sliced bananas. (2 or 3)

Filling:
Cream 1 8 oz. Philadelphia cream cheese
        3 cups fresh milk
        3 boxes instant vanilla pudding

Pour over bananas. Garnish with Cool Whip (large container). Refrigerate.

Ann Fagerroos

FLORIDA LIME PIE

1 can Eagle Brand condensed milk
½ cup fresh lime juice
3 eggs separated
1 pre-baked pie shell
1 cup whipping cream
Sugar to taste
1 tbsp. rum

Mix milk, lime juice & egg yolks. Beat egg whites separately and fold in above mixture. Bake at 250° for 10 minutes. Chill.

Whip cream and add sugar to taste (about 3 tbsp.) and rum. Spread over chilled pie filling. Sprinkle with powdered cinnamon. Keep refrigerated.

Luana McKenney

LIME JELLO CHIFFON PIE

Crust: 1½ cups flour and 1½ sticks butter. At room temperature. Mix until dough leaves sides of bowl. Form into a ball. Press into pie pan. Bake at 400° for 10 minutes or until golden brown.

Filling: 1 small box lime jello and ¾ cup boiling water.

Stir until completely dissolved – 2 to 3 minutes. Add 1 cup ice water. Continue to stir for 1 to 2 minutes. Chill immediately for ½ hour or until jello is shaky, not set.

In separate bowls: Beat 1 bottle Avoset. Beat 4 egg whites, adding ½ cup sugar slowly. Continue beating until egg whites form stiff peaks. Set aside.

Beat the chilled jello on medium for 1-2 minutes. Transfer to large bowl and add the beaten Avoset, folding slowly and carefully. Then add the egg whites delicately. Do not beat or stir. Fold carefully till ingredients are blended. Fill baked, cooled pie shell and chill for 3-4 hours.

Note: you may substitute any flavored jello. Do not use instant jello.

Belle Rogers

PAT AND PRESS CRUST – Custard Pie

1½ cups flour   1½ tsp. sugar
½ tsp. salt

Mix well.

2 tbsp. milk   ½ cup Wesson oil

Add to flour mixture. Mix well.

Pat and Press into a 9 inch pie plate.

Custard:
4 eggs   2½ cups milk
¼ tsp. salt   ½ cup sugar
1 tsp. vanilla

Scald milk. Add milk mixture to remaining ingredients. Pour into pie crust. Sprinkle lightly with nutmeg. Bake at 475° for 5 minutes. Reduce heat to 425° for 10 minutes. Reduce heat to 350° for 30 minutes (or until done).

Vi-Lani Robertson

CHOCOLATE PIE FILLING

1 cup (6 oz. pkg.) semi sweet chocolate bits
2 egg yolks   ½ cup sour cream
2 egg whites   ¼ tsp. salt
⅓ cup honey

Melt chocolate in top of double boiler. Add egg yolks and stir until mixture leaves side of pan. Remove from heat. Blend in cream, beat until smooth. Set aside.

Beat egg whites and salt until stiff but not dry. Add honey very slowly, beating well after each addition. Continue beating until it stands in stiff glossy peaks. Fold in chocolate mixture. Chill at least 2 hours.

Mae Barth

LEMON PIE

1 15 oz. can Eagle Brand milk   2 egg yolks
½ cup lemon juice   1 tsp. grated lemon rind

Blend all ingredients and pour into a graham cracker crumb shell. Chill overnight.

Mary Kirkham

CHOCOLATE MARVEL PIE

1 6 oz. pkg. semi sweet   3 eggs, separated
   chocolate bits   3 tbsp. milk
2 tbsp. sugar

Place chocolate chips, sugar, milk in saucepan and melt over low heat, stirring until smooth. Cool slightly. Add egg yolks one at a time, stirring after each.

Beat egg whites until stiff. Fold into the chocolate mixture. Pour into a baked pie shell.

Chill. Serve with whipped cream. Excellent and easy.

Olive Linde

LEMON CAKE PIE

1 cup sugar   Juice and rind of 1 lemon
3 tbsp. butter   1 unbaked 9 inch pie shell
½ cup milk, diluted with   3 tbsp. flour
   ½ cup water   2 eggs, separated

Combine sugar, flour and butter. Stir in beaten egg yolks. Add lemon juice, rind and diluted milk slowly. Beat egg whites stiff. Fold into mixture. Pour into unbaked pie shell. Bake at 350° 30 minutes or until firm.

Eleanor Azevedo

FILLING FOR LEMON PIE

This seems like a lot of work but the end result is worth your while as it is a tart filling. The recipe came from England with my grandmother.

3 lemons, juice and rind – 1½ cup plus 1 tbsp.	1 cup sugar
	1 cup water
3 tbsp. cornstarch	4 eggs (when scarce use 2)

Separate eggs. Cook juice, rind, water and sugar in double boiler. When hot add egg yolks slowly. Return to heat. Add cornstarch mixed with a little water and cook until clear.

Pour filling into a crust that has been cooled after baking.

Beat whites until stiff. Add 2 tbsp. sugar. Cover the top of the pie with this and brown in oven.

Jane Horn

THE NUTTIEST PIE

Crust: Mix thoroughly

⅓ cup shortening	1 cup flour
½ tsp. salt	

Sprinkle 3 tbsp. cold water over this mixture and stir gently until a ball is formed. It will be crumbly, but press into a firm ball in your hands and roll on floured surface to fit a 9 inch pie plate. Crimp edges. Press ¼ cup *finely* chopped roasted peanuts into crust and prick all over with fork. Bake at 425° for 15 minutes.

Custard Filling: Beat together

2 whole eggs	¾ cup white sugar
3 tbsp. cornstarch	Dash of salt

Add to 2 cups of milk in heavy saucepan. Cook, stirring constantly, until thickened. Remove from heat and add ⅓ cup peanut butter and 1 tbsp. vanilla. Cool thoroughly and pour into cooled crust. Chill in refrigerator. Before serving, cover with sweetened whipped cream and sprinkle with 2 tbsp. chopped peanuts.

Serves 6.

Bobbie Pope

KULOLO

2 medium-size Hawaiian taro (approximately 7 cups)
2 cups coconut milk (room temperature)
1 cup water (preferably coconut; tap water O.K.)
   at room temperature
1½ cups dark brown cane sugar
⅔ cup honey
9x11 cake pan
10 medium ti leaves
Aluminum foil, Fine vegetable grater

1. Peel taro.
2. Grate taro to fine or smooth texture.
3. Mix grated taro, being sure no pieces of ungrated taro are present.
4. Add coconut milk and water; mix well.
5. Add honey; mix well.
6. Add dark brown cane sugar and mix well.
7. Taste. Add more honey and sugar if desired.
8. Grease pan very lightly; line with foil so that 1 end is long enough to use as cover and ends tuck tightly around lip of pan.
9. Line foil with ti leaves on bottom of pan, being certain leaves overlap as well as rise up around pan edges about ½ inch. (Prepare leaves by removing center stem without tearing leaves)
10. Pour the entire mixture on ti leaves in pan and smooth out evenly.
11. Place 4 or 5 prepared ti leaves on mixture, tucking leaves carefully around edges of mixture. Cover with long end of foil being sure it is creased tightly around pan edges.
12. Bake in heated oven at 325° for 4½ hours. After 3 hours check to see that mixture is browning. After 4½ hours turn off oven and leave mixture in until oven cools. Kulolo is ready to eat.

Enjoy! Serves 10.

Reverend William Kaina, Pastor
Kawaiahaʻo Church, Honolulu
and Mama Kahu Sandy

AUNT GUSSIE'S CLOUD

6 egg yolks, 6 egg whites (separated)
¾ cup granulated sugar
¾ cup lemon juice

Beat egg yolks slightly and combine with lemon juice and sugar. Cook over hot water until consistency of custard.

Add 1 pkg. plain gelatin dissolved in ¼ cup of cold water. Remove from heat and add grated rind of 1 lemon.

In large mixing bowl, beat 6 egg whites until stiff, gradually add ¾ cup of granulated sugar. Fold custard into beaten egg whites.

Have ready a large angel food cake. Package mix makes the right size, or use a bakery angel cake.

Cover bottom of angel food cake pan with wax paper cut to fit. Put small amount of custard into pan, then alternate layers of broken pieces of cake with custard mixture. (There will probably be some cake left over.) Cover with wax paper. Chill 24 hours. When ready to serve, or some hours before, unmold, remove paper, and frost entire cake with 1 pint whipped cream. 10-12 servings.

This is a yummy dessert but not for calorie counters!

Maureen Shaw

EASY PEPPERMINT ICE CREAM

16 marshmallows
¾ cup crushed red and white peppermint sticks
½ pt. whipping cream
1 cup hot milk

Melt marshmallows in milk and let cool. Combine with stiffly whipped cream. Beat with beater until light and smooth, then fold in crushed peppermint candy. Pour in trays and freeze.

Helen V. Rantala

ORANGE PEACH JELLO MOLD

3 boxes orange jello   1 bottle Avoset whipping cream
1 #10 can of peaches, save juice

Dissolve orange jello in 2 cups hot water. Add juice from peaches. Add peaches.

After this has molded whip Avoset. With a large salad fork mix together until light and fluffy. Remold.

If you are going to use this at a party where it will stand at room temperature, add 1 more package gelatin to hold shape when unmolded. Makes 3 quarts.

Henry Piltz Kramer

PINEAPPLE MINT FREEZE

1 20 oz. can crushed pineapple
1 tbsp. unflavored gelatin
1 10 oz. jar mint jelly
1 cup whipping cream
1 tsp. confectioner's sugar

Drain pineapple, reserving syrup. Soften gelatin in syrup in saucepan. Add jelly. Heat until smooth. Stir in pineapple. Chill until mixture is thickened and syrupy. Whip cream with sugar. Fold into thickened gelatin. Spoon into loaf pan or jello mold. Freeze until firm. Let stand 10 minutes before serving. Unmold. Great for a hot day! Serves 12.

Elizabeth Hammer

AVOCADO MILK SHERBET

1 cup mashed avocado pulp   ⅛ tsp. salt
1¼ cups sugar   ½ cup pineapple juice
½ cup orange juice   ½ cup lime juice or
1 cup milk   ½ cup lemon juice

Mix together. Freeze. Yields 1¼ quarts.

Julia Toomey

KULOLO – TARO AND BROWN SUGAR PUDDING

1½ lbs. taro
2 tbsp. honey
Grated meat of 1 coconut

coconut milk
2 tbsp. molasses
Brown sugar to taste

Mix well 1½ lbs. grated raw taro with coconut milk and grated coconut. Add a little salt and enough brown sugar to take away the sharp biting taste of the taro. Add 2 or more tablespoons of honey and molasses. Bake slowly for 2-3 hours.

Julia Toomey

KO‘ELE PALAU – SWEET POTATO PUDDING

2½ lbs. sweet potatoes
¾ can condensed milk

1 can coconut milk

Steam the potatoes and peel when warm. Mash the potatoes while pouring in the coconut milk and the condensed milk. A little bit goes a long way. Serves 6-10.

Mollie Casil

BREAD PUDDING

2 loaves stale bread, torn up
1 tbsp. cinnamon
1 box seedless yellow raisins
1 small can chopped
  macadamia nuts

1 lge. can applesauce
3 green apples, peeled and
  sliced thin
1 tbsp. nutmeg
4 eggs

Mix all except apples. Moisten with water. Let stand. Spread into square baking pan. Top with apples. Bake at 400° for 1 hour. Serve.

Judith R. Parrish

BREADFRUIT AND COCONUT PUDDING

1½ cups coconut milk from
   1 grated coconut, with
1 cup boiling water

3 cups ripe breadfruit pulp
½ cup sugar
½ tsp. salt

Pour boiling water over grated coconut and allow to stand for 15 minutes. Knead the coconut with hands and strain through 2 thicknesses of cheesecloth, squeezing out as much milk as possible.

Scrape out the pulp from a soft ripe breadfruit and add coconut milk, salt and sugar. Pour into an oiled baking dish and bake 1 hour or more in a 350° oven. Yields 6 servings.

Julia Toomey

HAUPIA COCONUT PUDDING

3 tbsp. cornstarch
3 tbsp. sugar

½ tsp. salt
2 cups coconut milk

Combine dry ingredients. Add ½ cup of coconut milk and blend to a smooth paste. Heat remaining milk on low heat. Add cornstarch mixture, stirring constantly until thickened. Pour into shallow pan. Let it cool until firm. Yields 6 servings.

Julia Toomey

POI PU – PUMPKIN POI

1 bag Taro poi, 1 16 oz. can pumpkin. Use no water. Mix very well and serve.

Charlotte Clarke

MANGO COBBLER

In a saucepan boil for 5 minutes:

1 cup pineapple juice   2 cups sugar
1 tsp. almond extract   2 tbsp. orange liqueur

Crust: Mix

2 cups flour   ½ tsp. salt
½ tsp. baking powder   ½ cup butter
¼ cup sugar   ¼ to ½ cup milk

Mix together slowly. Do not make it thin, should be sticky and doughy. Roll out ½ inch thick. Put into oblong pan.

Peel 4 medium mangos. Rinse with cold water. Slice into pan with crust. Put in 2 cups pineapple. Pour fruit liquid over fruit. Put 4 dabs of butter on top of fruit. Sprinkle sugar and cinnamon on top. Bake at 350° for 35 minutes or until brown.

Topping for cobbler

½ pint whipping cream   ½ pt. sour cream
¼ cup sugar   1 tsp. almond extract
1 tsp. orange liqueur

Whip cream until thick. Whip sour cream in slowly. Add sugar slowly. Add extract and liqueur when ready to serve.

Cobbler can be served warm or cold. Sprinkle nutmeg on top of cream.

Ruth Bradford

SHERBET DESSERT

1 cup crushed pecan sandies
1 pt. whipping cream
3 tbsp. sugar

1 qt. sherbet such as lemon/
  lime/orange mixture
1 tsp. vanilla
1 cup chopped nuts

Whip cream. Add vanilla, sugar, cookies and nuts. Spread ½ inch thick in 9x13 pan. Cover with sherbet, then remainder of cookie mixture. Freeze overnight.

Jackie March

ORANGE DELITE

2 pkgs. orange jello
  (regular size)

2 cups boiling juice drained
  from fruit, plus orange juice
1 pt. orange sherbet

Dissolve jello in fruit juices. Stir in sherbet until dissolved. Refrigerate for 30 minutes to 1 hr. When cool and set like egg whites, add:

½ pt. Cool Whip
1 can Mandarin oranges

1 can pineapple, crushed

Pour into jello mold that has been brushed lightly with mayonnaise. Chill 4 hours or overnight. Remove from mold. Serves 8.

Barbara Livermore

BANANA-COCONUT CUSTARD

2 eggs
2 cups milk
3 cups fresh grated coconut

1 cup sliced very ripe bananas
1/16 tsp. salt
½ tsp. vanilla

Beat eggs slightly. Add other ingredients. Pour into a baking dish and bake in slow oven – 300°-325° for 1 hour. Yields 6 servings.

Julia Toomey

CARROT STEAMED PUDDING

1 tsp. cinnamon	⅔ cups oil
1 tsp. baking soda	1 tsp. nutmeg
1 cup grated carrot	1 cup flour
1 cup grated potato	1 cup sugar
1 cup raisins	1 cup walnuts

Mix all ingredients together. Place in steamer and cook for 1½-2 hours, checking water occasionally. Serve with whipped or unwhipped cream. Serve while hot. Serves about 24. Good at Christmas.

Mollie Casil

BANANA MILK SHAKE

1 very ripe eating banana	½ tsp. vanilla
1 cup fresh or diluted evaporated milk	⅛ tsp. salt

Choose a banana with skin flecked with brown spots or skin entirely brown. Peel and press through a coarse sieve. Add other ingredients gradually stirring with fork until well mixed. Chill thoroughly. Shake in a fruit jar and serve in a tall glass. For variety add 3 tbsp. guava juice and 1 tbsp. sugar. Makes 1 serving.

Julia Toomey

POI COCKTAIL

1 cup prepared poi	2 cups milk
1 cup vanilla ice cream	¼ cup red wine
½ cup sugar	Dash of nutmeg

Whip poi, ice cream and sugar until smooth. Add milk gradually, beating constantly. Blend in the wine and serve with nutmeg sprinkled over the surface. Yields 1 quart.

Julia Toomey

LEMON PUDDING

1 cup sugar
1 cup milk
2 eggs, separated

Grated rind and juice of 1 lemon
2 tbsp. butter
2 tbsp. flour

Blend sugar, butter and add beaten egg yolks. Add flour, lemon juice and rind. Add milk, fold in beaten egg whites. Bake in pan of water in 300° oven for 45 minutes.

Mae Barth

CHOCOLATE ZUCCHINI

½ cup soft margarine
1¾ cups sugar
1 tsp. vanilla

½ cup oil
2 eggs
½ cup buttermilk

Sift:
4 tbsp. Hershey cocoa
  (no sugar)
1 tsp. soda
½ tsp. cinnamon

2 cups grated zucchini
2½ cups flour
½ tsp. salt

Mix margarine, oil and sugar. Add eggs. Alternate dry ingredients and buttermilk. Add vanilla and zucchini. Pour into greased and floured cake pan. Bake at 325° for 35 to 40 minutes.

Vi-Lani Robertson

SHERRY TRIFLE

From England.
A favourite dessert of King Henry the Eighth

2 Layers of Sponge Cake (can substitute with 2 layers of yellow cake
    mix quite well).
Small amount of strawberry jam
1 can pears
1 packet of Bird's custard powder
1 pint milk
Sherry, dry, not sweet
Cherries and chopped walnuts (to decorate)
1 packet whipped topping

In a bowl (glass looks best) spread a thin layer of strawberry jam
over the bottom.

Place 1 layer of sponge cake in bowl and again spread thin layer of
jam onto sponge, then cover with a layer of very thin sliced pears.
Dribble small amount of sherry over pears. Cover with second layer
of sponge cake. Prick all over top with sharp fork, then slowly pour
⅔ cup (up to 1 cup if desired) of sherry over top layer. Let stand to
soak in, meanwhile making custard sauce (directions on packet).

Now place another layer of very thin pear slices over top layer. Next
pour the hot custard all over. Note: a knob of butter or margarine
stirred into custard will enhance flavour and prevent layer of skin
forming.

When cool place in refrigerator, preferably over night.

When ready to use, make up Dream Whip topping, spread all over
top, covering set custard. Finally decorate with the cherries and
nuts, dropping them onto the cream.

Trixi Sharman

CHERRY TARTS

2 8 oz. blocks cream cheese
2 eggs
¾ cup sugar
1 tbsp. each lemon juice and
vanilla

Vanilla wafers
Cup cake holders
Can cherry pie filling

Mix first 4 ingredients until fluffy and smooth. Spoon over wafers, placed on bottom of cup cake holders set in muffin pans. Bake 10-15 minutes at 375°. Spoon cherry filling over cooked mixture and refrigerate. Makes 24.

Eloise Naone

KANAWHA MUD (Named for a river in W. Va.)

¼ lb. butter
3 eggs
1 pt. heavy cream or 2 pkgs.
of Dream Whip

1 box graham cracker crumbs
1 cup sugar
1 14 oz. can crushed pineapple

Cream together butter and sugar until light and fluffy. Add eggs, 1 at a time, beating until lemon-colored. Stir in pineapple, drained thoroughly. In another bowl beat cream until it holds a point (or follow Dream Whip directions). Fold into pineapple mixture. Starting with crumbs, fill a baking dish with alternate layers of crumbs and pineapple mixture. Sprinkle chopped macadamia nuts on top. Chill at least 12 hours. Serves 12-15.

Mary Reed Hughes

KING KALĀKAUA'S CHAMPAGNE PUNCH

CHILL   6 bottles of champagne
2 bottles Sauterne (white Bordeaux wine, not too dry or heavy)

CHILL OVERNIGHT OR AT LEAST 5 HOURS.

POUR   into a large punch bowl

SLICE   6 lemons and 6 oranges. Add to bowl

ADD   6 mint leaves
Sliced peeled sticks of 1 ripe pineapple
1 Cup sugar

POUR   Sauterne and 3 bottles of the champagne into the ingredients in the punchbowl.

STIR   Until sugar melts

ADD   2 Cups brandy and 2 quarts fresh strawberries

MIX   Gently

BEFORE SERVING add the remaining 3 bottles of Champagne.

Ellen Vasconcellos
(Courtesy of the Daughters of Hawai'i)

AUNT ADDIE'S HARD SAUCE

¼ cup butter
2 tbsp. brandy (can substitute
vanilla or creme de cacao)

White of 1 egg
1 cup powdered sugar

Beat butter to cream, slowly add sugar. Beat until light. Add egg white and beat until light and frothy. Gradually add flavoring and beat again.

Heap on small dish and sprinkle lightly with nutmeg. Allow to harden in ice box.

This recipe is 100 years old and is still the best to go with mince and pumpkin pie.

Beverly Schulte

SAN FRANCISCO ZABAGLIONE (GENOVA STYLE)

6 tbsp. sugar
6 egg yolks plus white of 1 egg
6 half (egg) shell measures of Marsala Wine
¼ tsp. vanilla

Combine all in top of double boiler. Place over hot water and beat with whisk until frothy, smooth and slightly thick. Serve hot immediately. Serves 4 to 6.

Jeanne Read Alden

MARY'S HOLIDAY CHOCOLATE SAUCE

4 squares baking chocolate
1 stick butter
2 6 oz. cans Pet milk

1 pkg. confectioner's sugar
Pinch of salt
2 tsp. vanilla

Break up chocolate in top of double boiler. Melt chocolate and butter together. Stir in Pet milk and sugar. Continue to cook for 15 minutes. Add a pinch of salt (a good one!) and 2 tsp. vanilla.

Delicious served heated over good vanilla ice cream. Can be kept indefinitely in glass jar in refrigerator.

Luana McKenney

MAI TAI SUNDAE SAUCE

1 12 oz. jar pineapple/mango jam, or substitute peach jam
3 tbsp. butter
2 tsp. lime juice
¼ cup orange marmalade
½ tsp. each – cinnamon, cloves, nutmeg

Combine ingredients and cook over low heat until smoothly blended. Add ¼ cup rum.

Serve warm over ice cream (macadamia flavor is best). Bananas may also be added just before serving.

Dorothy Kendall

PINEAPPLE POLYNESIAN

Use with meat or as a hot dish for picnics and potlucks.

Saute in 2 tbsp. margarine: ¼ cup each chopped onions, chopped celery, green pepper.

Add: 2 cups pineapple chunks
3 tbsp. soy sauce
¼ tsp. ground cloves
1 mashed garlic clove
1 tbsp. brown sugar
¼ tsp. ground ginger or 1 tbsp. chopped fresh ginger
¼ cup vinegar
1 tbsp. cornstarch mixed in ½ cup water

Cook until thickened and clear.

Dorothy Kendall

COCKTAIL SAUCE FOR SEAFOOD

⅓ cup chili sauce
3 tbsp. prepared horseradish
4 tbsp. lemon juice
2 tsp. Worcestershire sauce
Ketchup
Dash of salt
A few dashes of Tabasco

Makes 1 cup - 6 servings.

David Lowman

BARBECUE SAUCE FOR TERIYAKI MEAT

1 cup shoyu
1½ cups sugar
1 tbsp. ajinomoto
1 pinch salt

Cook together. Cool. When cool add 1 finger of ginger, grated, and 1 or 2 cloves of garlic, grated.

Store for future use.

Soak thin slices of meat in the sauce for a few minutes. Pan fry with or without oil. Serve with hot rice.

Tsuroko A. Ohye

NO CAL GINGER DRESSING

Grate a large section of ginger root. Cover with 1 cup boiling water. Strain through cheesecloth.

Add equal parts of Japanese vinegar, sugar or Sweeta to taste. Use on lettuce and cucumber salad.

Henry Piltz Kramer

SISSY'S MUSTARD RING

1 tbsp. gelatin	½ pint heavy cream, whipped
4 well beaten eggs	½ cup cold water
⅔ cup apple cider vinegar	½ cup sugar
2 tbsp. dry mustard plus	
1 tbsp. cold water	

Mix gelatin and cold water. Let stand 5 minutes. Melt in top of double boiler. Set aside. Mix eggs, sugar and apple vinegar well and add to first mixture. Set aside. Make paste of mustard and 1 tbsp. of cold water. Add to other mixture. Cook till thickened. Cool and refrigerate to thicken further. Fold in whipped cream. Add a dash of salt and yellow food coloring. Delicious served with sliced ham.

Luana McKenney

MARINADE SAUCE (FOR LONDON BROIL)

1½ lbs. steak	1 clove garlic
¼ cup salad oil	1 tsp. black pepper
2 tbsp. lemon juice	1 tsp. celery salt
2 tbsp. shoyu	2 tbsp. green onion

Mix ingredients in long shallow pan. Place steak in pan for a couple of hours or even a half a day. This helps to tenderize meat. Broil each side for about 3 minutes for rare. Slice across grain.

Add more lemon juice if desired, for tasty lemon steak.

Flodie Van Orden

SCRUMPTIOUS TURKEY DRESSING

4 onions, chopped
4 cups chopped celery
  and leaves
½ cup corn meal (optional)

¾ cup margarine
1 cup raw cashews

It is not necessary to add any liquid. Simmer all ingredients together. Combine and add:

1½ cups chopped parsley
2 loaves bread, cubed
  (4½ qts.)
3 eggs, beaten lightly
1 tbsp. salt

1 tbsp. sage, or more to taste
  (optional)
1 cup pecans
½ tbsp. pepper

Stuff lightly into turkey. Roast and enjoy!

Ample for a 15-18 lb. turkey.

David Lowman

CORNBREAD DRESSING FOR CHICKEN OR TURKEY

4 cups crumbled cornbread made with white cornmeal
2 cups dry bread crumbs
3½ cups chicken stock
3 eggs
1 cup chopped celery
¼ cup chopped parsley

2 tsp. salt
½ tsp. pepper
1 chopped onion
1 tbsp. poultry seasoning

Mix cornbread and bread crumbs. Add stock. Beat eggs slightly, add salt and pepper. Add to bread mixture. Then add chopped celery, poultry seasoning, parsley and chopped onion. Turkey can be stuffed with dressing or bake it separately in a well-greased pan at 425° for 30-40 minutes.

Stuffs an 18 lb. turkey.

Mary Bennett

GRANDMOTHER'S FRENCH DRESSING

1 cup olive oil (Wesson will do) 1 cup white vinegar ½ cup catsup	1 tsp. salt ½ cup sugar 1 tbsp. onion juice 1 tsp. paprika

Shake well in glass jar. Makes about 1 pint.

Jean St. John

PREPARED MUSTARD

2 tsp. dry mustard 2 tsp. sugar	2 tsp. flour Pinch of salt

Mix with enough hot water to make a stiff paste. Add vinegar to thin for the table. Great with ham. Makes about ¼ cup.

Jean St. John

MOM'S TABLE MUSTARD

Do first – Vinegar Mix:

1 cup vinegar 1 med. onion, chopped	1 clove garlic, smashed 1 sm. chili pepper, chopped

Mix above ingredients and let boil for 5 minutes. Cool then strain and use liquid in making mustard.

3 tbsp. dry mustard 1 tbsp. sugar 2 tsp. flour	1 egg 1 tsp. olive or Wesson oil 1 tsp. salt

Mix dry ingredients until well blended. Then add egg and mix until smooth. Add boiled vinegar mix and stir until smooth. Bring to gentle boil and cook for 3 minutes – stirring constantly.

Remove from stove. Stir in the oil. Stir to work oil in. Bottle and seal with wax. Will keep for 6 months.

Yvonne Ernst

MANGO CHUTNEY

50 half-ripe or green (2 shopping bags full) mangoes. Peeled, cut up and salted. Let stand overnight. Rinse, drain and dry.

10 lbs. white sugar	1 bottle pickled ginger, use juice
3 lbs. grated fresh ginger	1½ qts. white vinegar
2 lge. onions	1 whole garlic bulb

Cook all these together until it begins to thicken 3-4 hours.

When thick and boiling, ½ hour before taking off stove add:

4 boxes white or golden raisins	2 tbsp. allspice
3 tbsp. nutmeg	2 tbsp. ground cloves

Place in sterile bottles. Add wax and seal. Makes 30 jars.

Henry Piltz Kramer

FRED'S PICKLED ONIONS

1 cup rice vinegar	1 tbsp. sugar
2 tsp. salt	¼ tsp. ajinomoto
Chili pepper (optional)	

Peel and cut onions in halves or fourths. Place in bottle.

Boil rest of ingredients and pour over onions while hot. Let cool and place in refrigerator. Eat in 2-3 days. 2 cups makes 1 quart jar, generous.

Mae Barth
(Courtesy of Fred Shimabukuro)

NOTES

POULTRY

SEAFOOD

VEGETABLES

CASSEROLES AND
ONE DISH MEALS

BREADS

COOKIES

CAKES

PIES

DESSERTS

MISCELLANEOUS:

GLOSSARY

Ajinomoto . . . . .M.S.G., Monosodium glutamate, Accent

Coconut Milk . . . . .Grated coconut, water added and coconut meat squeezed to make milk

Ginger Root . . . . .Root of ginger plant, may substitute ginger powder but the flavor will not be as distinct.

Hawaiian Salt . . . . .Coarse salt

Japanese vinegar, rice vinegar . . . . .Vinegar, sweeter, not as strong as regular type

Lau Lau . . . . .Package of Ti leaves containing pork, beef, salted fish or chicken with taro leaves and steamed.

Limu . . . . .Seaweed

Long Rice . . . . .Bean threads, long rice

Luau leaves . . . . .Taro plant leaves (or spinach leaves)

Lup Chong . . . . .Chinese sausage

Mochiko . . . . .Flour made from glutenous rice

Nori . . . . .Dried seaweed pressed into sheets

Poi . . . . .Made from cooked and pounded Taro corms. Use fresh, powder form, or bottled

Pupu . . . . .Appetizer

Shoyu . . . . .Soy Sauce

Taro . . . . .Polynesians' most important starchfood. Corms cooked for poi, tender leaves, called luau are similar to spinach.

Ti leaves . . . . .Plant. The leaves, lau ki, had a variety of uses, from packages for cooking and carrying, plates, raincoats and sandals.

Tofu . . . . .Soy bean curd

Wasabi powder . . . . .Japanese mustard, like horse radish

Won Ton Pi . . . . .Noodle paste squares

BOOK ORDER FORM:
THE FRIENDS OF 'IOLANI PALACE "COOK BOOK"

I wish to order _____ copies @ $10.00 $ _____
(PRICE INCLUDES ALL POSTAGE AND HANDLING)

Check or money order must be included with order.

Checks made payable and sent to:

The Palace Shop
c/o Iolani Palace
P.O. Box 2259 • Honolulu, Hawaii 96804
TELEPHONE (808) 522-0833

THE FRIENDS OF 'IOLANI PALACE
Cook Book

Ka Piko Pua o Hale Ali'i
King's Flower Vase

Purchaser's Name _____
(PLEASE PRINT)

Address _____

_____
(zip)

Telephone (   ) _____ Date _____

Purchaser's Signature _____

BOOK ORDER FORM:
THE FRIENDS OF 'IOLANI PALACE "COOK BOOK"

I wish to order _____ copies @ $10.00 $ _____
(PRICE INCLUDES ALL POSTAGE AND HANDLING)

Check or money order must be included with order.

Checks made payable and sent to:

The Palace Shop
c/o Iolani Palace
P.O. Box 2259 • Honolulu, Hawaii 96804
TELEPHONE (808) 522-0833

THE FRIENDS OF 'IOLANI PALACE
Cook Book

Ka Piko Pua o Hale Ali'i
King's Flower Vase

Purchaser's Name _____
(PLEASE PRINT)

Address _____

_____
(zip)

Telephone (   ) _____ Date _____

Purchaser's Signature _____